The Handbook of Incentive Compensation

The Handbook of Incentive Compensation

Rich Armstrong
Brad Hams
Cathy Ivancic
Loren Rodgers
Corey Rosen

The National Center for Employee Ownership
Oakland, California

This publication is designed to provide accurate and authoritative information in regard to the subject matter covered. It is sold with the understanding that the publisher is not engaged in rendering legal, accounting, or other professional service. If legal advice or other expert assistance is required, the services of a competent professional person should be sought.

Legal, accounting, and other rules affecting business often change. Before making decisions based on the information you find here or in any publication from any publisher, you should ascertain what changes might have occurred and what changes might be forthcoming. The NCEO's Web site (including the members-only area) and newsletter for members provide regular updates on these changes. If you have any questions or concerns about a particular issue, check with your professional advisor or, if you are an NCEO member, call or email us.

The Handbook of Incentive Compensation
Book design by Scott S. Rodrick

The National Center for Employee Ownership
1736 Franklin Street, 8th Floor
Oakland, CA 94612
(510) 208-1300
(510) 272-9510 (fax)
Web site: www.nceo.org

ISBN-10: 1-932924-64-7
ISBN-13: 978-1-932924-64-0

Contents

Preface

Corey Rosen
Executive Director, The National Center for Employee Ownership

Incentive plans are common in companies, but satisfaction with them is not. Surveys of human resource executives consistently show that incentive plans often do not live up to results.

It seems obvious enough. If employees have a stake in how well their company does, they will be more engaged and work more effectively, but there are endless articles and books about how to get your incentive plan to work well and thousands of consultants specializing in incentive plan design, often with their own unique plans. If getting the plan right were easy, there would be much less of a market for both the books and the consulting. Of course, it is not simple. Some researchers, in fact, have concluded that incentive plans do little incentivizing and may create more problems than they solve.

There are many reasons for this. First, incentive plan theory rests on the assumption that we make decisions about work effort based largely, or even solely, on rational economic calculations of what's in it for us. It turns out that we work the way we do for all kinds of reasons, including professional pride, intrinsic interests and personalities, group dynamics, our self-image, management behaviors, and many other factors.

Second, our economic calculations are not so rational after all. We misperceive risk, undervalue long-term rewards relative to short-term pay, place "irrational" value on how fairly rewards are divided, are more concerned about a dollar lost than a dollar gained, and more. All this complexity makes it tough to dangle the right carrots in the right way.

Third, work is just as complicated as we are. Even if incentives get people to do more of x, they may do it at the expense of y. They may improve quality but reduce output, improve individual performance but not cooperate as much with other employees, increase profits but take resources away from future growth, take imprudent risks for short-term gains at the expense of long-term success (think Wall Street and sub-prime mortgages), and make many other costly tradeoffs.

Still, too many companies report too much success with incentive compensation to just give up on the concept. In the decades of work the NCEO has done on employee ownership plans, one of the most powerful incentive tools, we have also learned a great deal about non-employee ownership models that work consistently well. In this book, we have drawn that experience together.

In the chapters that follow, I start off with an overview of why incentive plans do not always succeed. That is followed by a chapter by Loren Rodgers of the NCEO describing general principles on how to design an incentive plan and provide it the support needed to make it work. Brad Hams of Ownership Thinking provides a detailed description of an effective profit sharing plan. Cathy Ivancic of Workplace Development looks at other forms of short-term incentives, especially in the context of employee ownership plans. Rich Armstrong of the Great Game of Business writes about the exceptionally effective strategy developed at SRC Holdings that combines employee involvement and open-book management. Finally, I look at the various mechanisms (options, ESOPs, phantom stock, and so on) to provide equity incentives to employees.

CHAPTER 1

Why Incentive Pay Plans Fail

Corey Rosen

In his book *Parentnomics, An Economist Dad Looks at Parenting,* John Gans writes about how economic theories can apply to child rearing. Applying the concepts early on, he told his toddler that if he kept his diaper dry overnight, he'd get an award. After Gans left, the toddler simply took the diaper off. He soaked the bed—but the diaper was dry.

Recounting this story in a staff meeting, one of our staffers with young children said her husband had offered their young son a trip to the donut restaurant if he kept his diaper dry all night. In the morning, toddler #2 was still wearing his diapers and they were dry, but the incentive did not really work in this case either: toddler #2 wet his diapers every day for the next several weeks. The father could have offered donuts every day, of course, but that would create more problems (and hence the need to new incentives to eat better otherwise). The reward in this case would no longer be an incentive, but an entitlement.

These two stories illustrate two central problems of trying to induce behavior through economic incentives. The first toddler did what was needed to get the reward, but not what was needed to meet the overall objective (staying dry overnight). The second toddler accomplished the objective, but then saw no reason to do it again for no reward.

All of us who are parents—or who have been children—understand the perils of reward systems. Parents who tell their kids they can get desert if they clean their plate, pediatricians tell us, may end up with kids who eat more than they really need to eat and who view vegetables as obstacles to overcome. Growing up, there were rewards for who could read the most books over the summer. A logical response was to read lots of short ones quickly rather than longer, perhaps better, books more carefully. Student and professional athletes get rewarded in intangible and often very tangible ways for outstanding individual performance, measured by personal "stats." But that may mean not doing hard-to-measure things that could help the team.

Whether in parenting, sports, or at work, getting incentives right is very difficult. There are several key problems:

- Focusing on what the incentive is designed to encourage (quality, output, safety, etc.) at expense of doing other things that may also need doing.
- Where rewards are individualized, focusing on what helps you look good, not what is best for your team.
- Where rewards are team-based, focusing on what works for the team, but not the company.
- Reducing work to a pure dollars-and-cents calculation rather than something that can provide intrinsic satisfaction through accomplishment, achieving common goals, solving problems, suggesting ideas, and learning.
- Encouraging people to make an effort only when there is a reward. It is logical to cut back on effort if a reward is withdrawn if you believe that one might then be offered to get you to change.
- Employees may come to expect to get rewards every year. When goals aren't met, they will be demotivated much more than they ever were motivated by the incentive.

One response to these problems is that the incentives need to be more global. They need to get people to focus on overall corporate goals. Company-wide bonuses or profit sharing are ways to do that. But critics of these systems say that they do not give employees a sufficient line of sight between what they do and what they get as a reward.

The response to this from advocates of incentives is that getting incentive pay right requires a lot of thought and work and, if they are consultants, often their advice. Incentives need to balance various needs by creating measures that require that multiple objectives at the individual, group, and/or corporate level are all achieved. An incentive system, for instance, might provide additional pay to a team if its production numbers meet a certain target while quality and safety stay above a certain level. Or they might rely more on a system that assigns fully allocated costs to each operational activity and then determines what an improvement in some value added measure would create above these costs. The difficulty here is that these systems sometimes end up with Rube Goldberg-like charts that people find hard to understand.

It's also easy to confuse incentive pay with reward pay. The annual Christmas turkey is a reward, not an incentive. More seriously, the annual bonus declared by the board or management based on what employees see as some opaque process of divination sends out no clear measure of just what people are supposed to do to earn it.

This chapter explores these issues in more detail. I am not an implacable opponent of incentive pay. I have seen it work very effectively. But getting it right is tricky and probably requires making a fair number of mistakes along the way. Surveys of HR directors consistently show that most do not think their incentive systems are working as well as they should. Incentive pay must also never be seen as the simple—and simplistic—solution to creating an effective organization. That takes broader cultural changes, such as open-book management and systems for employees to have more input into and control over their own work.

Is Incentive Pay Based on the Wrong Way of Thinking About People?

The classical explanation of why incentive pay is a good idea is based on, surprise, classical economics. That is what we learned in school if we took an economics course. It's based on the idea of "economan." Economan (or econowoman—economists don't make gender distinctions) is a very convenient creature who makes theories and formulas work out very neatly for his parents, classical economists. Economan makes rational calculations about the economic value of everything he does. Offer me another dollar, he thinks, and I will make up to a dollar's worth of effort (but no more!). If the dollar is not paid today, he'll agreeably take a somewhat larger number of dollars in the future. How many dollars reflects how certain the reward is and the time value of the deferral. In his eyes, an extra dollar won is the same as an extra dollar lost. He'll be happy to earn a few extra bucks even if it means other people will get a lot more that they don't deserve (he won't begrudge a CEO's pay, no matter how high, if his pay goes up too). And if the reward is for a group, he'll happily "free ride" if he thinks that the efforts of others will suffice to get the maximum reward available.

Unfortunately, economan does not live on this planet. Or maybe it's not unfortunate, except to economic theorists: an economy filled economen would be a real mess. If people rely only on calculations of value maximization to make decisions, research has shown, they have a terrible time making any decision at all (imagine all the time poor economan would have to spend visiting endless Web sites to find the very best possible deal on a new television).

Humans are much more complicated creatures. A new school of thinking called behavioral economics looks at how people actually make decisions, not how they "rationally" should if they were economen. There are several key findings important for incentive pay:

- *People value losses much more than gains.* Researchers have found that when people gamble, if they win a certain amount (say $100), they are much less likely to take a double or nothing bet than if they lose $100. That same logic, in the real world, makes people hold on to stocks that have lost the same amount of money as stock that have made money. Losses are simply more painful to people than gains are rewarding. That means that incentive pay is also a lot more painful when not received than motivating when it is received.
- *People overvalue short-term income over long-term.* One hundred dollars paid a year from now, if fairly certain, should seem a lot better than $50 paid today, but most people will take the money now, thank you (that is why it is so difficult to get people to put more into a 401(k) plan even though the $100 they get in pay would be $150 or so in their 401(k), often be matched with more, and earn tax free returns over time). So incentive pay may work better if paid out frequently, but this may make people focus too much on short-term cost-cutting strategies that imperil long-term performance.
- *People are very intense about fairness.* If two people are told they can divide $10, but have to agree to the terms a second party sets for how it is divided, they will readily agree to a 50-50 or 60-40

split and maybe even a 70-30, but rarely will they go along with 80-20 or less, even it means neither ends up with anything. Most Harvard Business School students say they would prefer to make $75,000 when their peers make $50,00 than $100,000 when their peers make $125,000 (assuming dollars buy the same amount in each scenario). At work, this means incentive pay focused on "top performers" (as now commonly recommended by compensation consultants) is bound to create ill will among almost everyone else. They'll see it as unfair, especially given that surveys show that about 70% of us believe we are in the top 10% of performers in our group. But if we then shift to a more egalitarian approach, people may well see that as unfair too because, after all, they did more to deserve it.

- *People have a hard time valuing risk.* In general, people excessively discount the value of any reward if there is uncertainty attached. How often do you hear people say about an employee ownership plan that they consider it to be worth pretty much nothing because you never really can be sure it will pay out? Paradoxically, they also are too dazzled by the chance for a huge payout even if the chances of achieving it are infinitesimal (hence the super lotto). This creates a conflict. A company could dangle a very large reward for a huge stretch goal or smaller rewards for very certain ones, but neither is ideal.
- *We work for a lot of reasons besides money.* Ironically, academics are prime examples of this. In my former academic days, there was no end of complaints among my colleagues about how much more they could make if they had used their graduate school time to pursue a more lucrative career. We work to achieve something, to give us something to do, to be part of a community on the job, to learn and advance, to meet challenges, and much more. We are as much or more motivated at work by these intrinsic factors as by money. Alfie Kohn, a primary critic of incentive pay, argued that because of this, basing pay systems on incentives is inherently demeaning to people. The intrinsic value of work, and our desire to get along with colleagues, is part of why the so-called "1/n" problem (the more people in the group divide a reward, no matter how large,

the less people will see an individual need to do anything) turns out to be largely a myth.

Incentive design has largely failed to integrate the new research by behavioral economics. To help you make the most of this new field's insights, the rest of this chapter focuses on seven common challenges in designing incentive plans and suggests some solutions.

Key Problem 1: Incentivizing What?

The first, and usually most important, problem is deciding what to incentivize. Say a company has a problem with product quality. Managers could provide a bonus for improving it, but would workers then be much too careful at the risk of slowing production to an unprofitable point? This is a "toddler number one" problem—they get the specific behavior requested, but at the expense of the real goal. Maybe it should be a reward for maximizing production, but only if quality stays above a certain minimum level. But what if that means that an employee with a promising new idea for changing the way the process works finds it shot down because, short-run anyway, it will lower production? This is like paying toddler number two donuts for every dry diaper—it accomplishes the goal, but at the expense of larger purposes.

The solution to this usually is to come up with some mix of incentives. A common approach is for there to be a profit sharing plan to keep the focus on a larger goal, an employee ownership plan to focus on a longer-term goal, and some kind of short-term reward for meeting a specific goal based on the individual or, more commonly, the group's key issues. The sort-term incentive can fairly easily be tweaked and improved without endangering the other rewards, making any losses associated with changes less painful.

For instance, a company might decide that it would allocate costs to each function and give a quarterly bonus for lowering the costs relative to units of output, provided a minimum quality standard is maintained. A customer service function could get bonuses for reductions in complaints or retention of customers who make complaints. Accounts payable could get a reward for keeping payment time for bills below a certain level.

Problem 2: Maxing Out

A problem with the kinds of short-term bonuses described above is that employees may reach a level where incremental improvement is difficult. If incentives are based on beating an ever-improving standard of performance, you'll have the "taken away entitlement" problem. It may be that ever-increasing performance is not needed. Just staying at a good level may suffice.

A different approach is suggested by Springfield ReManufacturing Company, progenitors of the Great Game of Business concept (described in detail in this book in Rich Armstrong's chapter). Each year, new critical numbers are chosen that address a key concern at the company and/or work group level. Employees earn bonuses for reaching target numbers. The bonus pays significant dollars for meeting company goals and more fun rewards for short-term group goals. Simple enough so far. But the key insight of the Great Game process is open-book management and employee participation make employees really feel like they "own" the numbers (and, in this case, they actually own the company too). When employees who feel ownership solve a problem, it stays solved and a new problem can be addressed. That's because the solution is not usually more effort, it better ideas for a different way to do things.

Problem 3: Overcoming Complexity

At the outset, I said that one solution to the excessive focus that incentives create on limited goals is to create more complex formulas that account for many goals. But that complexity itself is a problem because it is hard to understand the formulas.

The Great Game approach can help here too. You actually don't have to try to solve every problem at once. If quality is a major concern, focus on fixing it, albeit educating employees about how much quality may be too much. When better systems for that are in place, focus on how production can grow within that quality control system.

A different solution is used by Web Industries Hartford, another employee owned company. Rather than ignoring complexity, Michael Quarrey, the plant manager, embraced it by setting up a Kaizen process.

Kaizen is a demanding but effective system in which employees—all employees—periodically spend up to a few days taking apart an entire work process, charting how work flows, how much cost and revenue is attributable to each element, and brainstorming ideas for improvement. By understanding how everything fits together, and having the chance to change it, employees can come to see the bonus as an appropriate reward for continuous improvement. They can deal with the complexity because they have all invested time to understand it intimately.

Problem 4: Short-Termism

The excessive undervaluing of long-term rewards is one of the most frustrating things to companies that share ownership, but even those with annual profit sharing may find that employees are focused on the very short now. Part of the solution has to be education and involvement. The more people understand the numbers and use them at work, the more they will identify with the company and its long-term possibilities. Another partial solution can be combining short- and long-term rewards, as described above. A third way have an annual profit sharing formula, but it is paid out quarterly. To avoid paying profits early that later losses may force them to rescind, a "10-20-30-40" formula is used in which 10% of the potential future profit pool projected for the year is paid out in the first quarter, 20% in the second, and so on.

Problem 5: It's Just Not Fair

This may well be the toughest problem of all. In one corner, we have the undisputed masters of the universe (in their view, anyway) who know their contributions are more essential than their peers (self-perceived masters exist at every level in the company). In corner two, we have the huddled masses who just get by every day.

That, at least, is the common view of compensation consultants these days who are especially find of quoting the "80-20" rule that 80% of the effects come from 20% of the causes, including productivity at work. The 80-20 rule was created by an early 20th century economist Vilfredo Pareto to describe land ownership in Italy. Decades later, an organizational development consultant said it must apply to companies too, and it became an urban legend, widely believed, not only never proven, but actually disproven. A popular variant is the 70-20-10 rule pioneered at GE that sates that 10% of your people need to be fired every year, 20% given the most rewards, and 70% just maintained. Enron had a similar system, and researchers found one result was that managers hired people so they could fire them the next year to protect their existing colleagues.,

The theory here (and it has some merit) is that if top performing people perceive they are not getting enough of the incentive pie, they will stop performing so well or just leave. The problems are legion, however, and well documented. Focusing most incentives on the top people (80% of the incentive pool to the 20% of the people would be a common suggestion) tells the 80% they are not much valued, creating a self-fulfilling prophecy. People also will be reluctant to cooperate or share credit, much less actually help someone else succeed, even if the business overall would benefit. Finally, every company is different. Some, hopefully yours, have a great many more top performers at their jobs. I know as far as I am concerned, for instance, all of the NCEO staff is at the very top of their game.

So is the solution to just divide incentives equally or based on relative pay? Those are very common approaches, especially the latter. The argument is that pay is a reasonable reflection of people's value to the company, and that incentives should follow that. The difficulty here is that because most people believe they are top performers, a lot of people towards the bottom of your pay scale may feel cheated. On the other hand, people near the top of your pay scale may feel cheated if incentives are divided equally. The fact is, there is a logical, principled argument for both approaches: you will need to say explicitly to people why you chose one argument and rejected the other.

If merit-based incentives are used, it is essential that people buy into how the assessments are made. If they see them as political, inaccurate, or otherwise biased, you create more problems than you solve. Focus groups and surveys may give you good feedback on this; alternatively, you can get employees at all levels involved in creating the system. That way, even if it is not perfect, it will nonetheless be seen as more fair. The perfect may be the enemy of the widely accepted good.

Problem 6: Not Just Rewards—Incentives

There's a difference. Incentives change people's behavior; rewards are a gift that have no clear link to behavior. What some companies think of as incentive pay is really just a reward that, if ever taken away, will create hard feelings that more than outweigh any good it once did. That's a very apt critique of a lot of systems that people call incentives.

Employees just see some bonus periodically paid out because the board or management declares them, but the link between behavior and bonus happens behind the scenes, so it's impossible for employees to make the connection. There is no incentive effect here. The bonuses may engender greater loyalty and team camaraderie, but that's because people like gifts.

Problem 7: It's Not Just the Money

Finally, remember it is not all about money. Recognition is an important reward (but it may be empty if that is all there is). Small fun rewards like going out to a ball game or dinner after meeting some short-term goal can disproportionately motivating. Most important, the process matters. Open book and high employee involvement management are very important motivators for a lot of people. They are not enough on their own, however. Just giving people a "sense of ownership" is about as satisfying as a "sense of lunch"—that pie sure smells good, doesn't it? But don't touch! Only I get a piece. Real ownership and rewards make the effort to be effectively involved seem like a lot more than just management manipulation for the benefit of other shareholders.

Conclusion

Incentive pay is very tricky. There are no magic bullets, no perfect formulas. Each company has to find what works for its own structure, workforce, and culture. Find out what other people do through conferences and networks. Get employees involved in designing and monitoring the system. Make changes when needed. And, perhaps, for some companies, just conclude no system is better than anything you can figure out. If you can find a system that works for you, incentive pay can be a transformative process.

CHAPTER 2

Designing and Supporting Effective Incentive Systems

Loren Rodgers

Incentive programs are dangerous. They always have unintended consequences, and some of them do more harm than good. The cause of the problems with incentive systems is that companies need to balance conflicting goals for the incentive systems. In the last chapter, Corey Rosen looked at some of the problems for the concept of incentive plans. But there are specific problems related to how incentive formulas are calculated as well. Companies face a number of dilemmas, including:

- Formulas or manager judgment? Some companies adopt a rigid bonus formula that lets people calculate the amount of their own bonuses, while others leave room for managers to allocate rewards among their own employees in order to recognize valuable employees whose contributions may not show up in performance data.
- Individual or group? Some companies reward star employees; others believe that individual rewards undermine teamwork.
- Big rewards or small? In order to maximize the effect of incentives, some companies pay substantial bonuses relative to compensation; others pay a more symbolic amount.
- Clear target or big picture? If the company breaks down performance targets to give each employee an individualized target that's simple and clearly within the field of influence of his or her job, then incentives based on that target may motivate behavior more

than a more distant goal like company-wide profitability. On the other hand, individualized and localized goals do not encourage teamwork, and they may distract people from other performance measures essential to the company.

While each company should build its own incentive program, in our experience there actually are good solutions to many of these dilemmas.

The Design of Effective Incentive Systems

Before we talk about good incentive systems, let's start with the other kind. Imagine yourself as an employee in Company X. Christmas is getting closer, and you've started wondering what kind of a bonus you might get this year. You start reading tea leaves: the floor is busy, there's that new guy, Joe, in the sales office, and there are rumors that the President has been playing golf regularly with the buyer for your company's largest customer. Sounds good! And you feel like you're in pretty good shape yourself: you fixed that workflow problem back in March, you've only been late once, and your supervisor has seemed more friendly lately than usual.

Now suppose the bonus shows up, and it's $50. You were expecting $500. You're angry and disappointed, so you talk with your supervisor, who says that you did a fine job but things are a bit tight at the company. You're not sure if you believe him, especially since Angie in accounting was looking pretty pleased when she opened her bonus check. You start thinking back over the past year: Was there something bad that you've forgotten? Did someone pin the blame for his own mistake on you? Is your supervisor a little too friendly with that new hire? You're focused on the past and completely unsure what you need to do in the future to make sure you get a better bonus.

Or suppose the check is actually $1,000. You're delighted, and you feel good about all the hard work you put in over the last year. So you keep showing up at work, doing the same job you've been doing, and hoping for the same bonus. The bonus may increase your loyalty to the company, but it hasn't conveyed any information or given you a reason to learn how to do your job more effectively.

This hypothetical bonus system violates some key principles—incentive systems should be driven by a formula, tied to company-wide goals, integrated with your information-sharing systems, and built on your employee education program.

The Conditional Promise

Here's the implicit message in discretionary bonus programs: "because of what you did and company performance last year, here's some money." Many companies don't do a great job of saying what exactly it was about last year's work that led to the bonus, and many others don't do much to keep employees informed about company performance. Those are two common problems with discretionary bonuses, but they aren't inevitable. What *is* an inevitable problem with discretionary bonuses is that they look backward, and people cannot change their past behavior. Discretionary bonuses can change employees' perception of the past (maybe it really was a good year after all), but even if your company shares information fanatically, past bonuses are unlikely to be a good predictor of next year's bonuses, and if you want to have an impact on how people are working right now, you need them to be focused on the future.

A simple tool to focus people on the future is the conditional promise. At its simplest, a conditional promise is an if-then statement: "if the company reaches goal X by the end of the year, then you will receive Y." A conditional promise inherently focuses on the future because a future condition must be satisfied before the promise comes into effect. This conditionality is powerful. As an employee, to the extent that I can help achieve X, I can help myself attain Y. Suddenly I have been empowered to have an impact on my own work-related future.

Conditional promises do more than orient people toward the future. Since "goal X" is almost invariably some measure of the company's performance in the market, the conditional promise focuses people where they should be focused: on concrete operational results that determine company profitability. A discretionary bonus makes employees think about how to make their supervisors like them. The company hopes that they will try to do that by doing the very best job they can, but some will decide that they are more likely to increase their bonuses by schmoozing their bosses, and that can have some disastrous side effects. Maybe I decide that I'll make myself look relatively good by making other people look relatively bad and undermine the effectiveness of my coworkers. Maybe my supervisor will propose a really stupid idea and I'll decide that it's in my interest to support that idea to look loyal. But even if your company doesn't suffer these perverse effects of a discretionary bonus, you're still shifting people's attention away from the marketplace and toward interpersonal dynamics.

Conditional promises change all that. Suddenly I'm not competing with the person in the next office or on the other machine for a share of a mysterious bonus pool. Instead, the market has reached into the work place and given me a reason to care what this month's gross margin looks like, whether we get the bid written this week or next, or what the defect rate is. I'm competing against the corporate goals, just like everyone else at the company: we are working together to succeed collectively, whether that means controlling cost, having a quiet conversation with an underperforming coworker, or letting my supervisor know that his idea probably is not too smart. This chapter has information about the owners' bonus, a terrific incentive system at Reflexite Corporation that is a conditional promise. Reflexite's former CEO Cecil Ursprung says the goal of the incentive program is to "replicate the system of American entrepreneurship" inside the company.

There is a downside, of course. Conditional promises are fragile. Conditional promises have no impact if employees lack faith in any part of the if-then statement. They may think it's simply impossible for the company to reach X, or they may doubt they personally can have any impact on attaining X, in which case any effort they might invest is wasted. They might see Y as insignificant, or they may doubt that they will really receive Y as a result of attaining X, in which case the incentive program does not provide any incentive. They may assume that they will receive Y whether or not X happens and decide to "free ride" on the hard work of their co-workers. Uncertainty about future company performance, the role of the broader market, risk aversion, natural skepticism, and gloomy news articles increase the odds that some employees will have little confidence in that promise.

Formula-Driven

This chapter discusses companies that have taken other approaches with great success, but in general we believe that the best way to address this fragility is to make your incentive system formula-driven. Lock your company into an incentive system that takes the discretion out of the system and replaces it with a predictable and transparent formula that determines who gets what, and you will find employees shifting their focus more to the future and more to concrete measures of success in the market.

Take a few critical numbers, one of which is usually some measure of profit, and put them into a formula. We'll talk more about how to do that later in this chapter, but the key is to make sure everyone in the company can easily find the formula, easily track the indicators that drive the formula, and knows which ones they can affect. In a formula-driven system, people still get their bonus check for past performance, but they know at the beginning of the year what they need to do in order to get that bonus. The formula, as long it is widely understood, helps give credibility and impact to the conditional promise.

Psychologists who study employee motivation say that predictability is the root of organizational trust. The simplest way for a company's compensation system to be predictable, of course, is not to use an incentive system at all—that way I know how much I'll earn from the company, under any condition except bankruptcy. For companies that don't want to promise exactly *how much* an employee's compensation will be, the next most predictable method is to promise exactly *how* the amount of compensation will be determined, and that means a formula. The key point about formula-driven bonuses is that people can see the chain of connection from their actions to the company's bottom-line performance, and then from company performance to their own bonus. Adopting and maintaining a transparent and predictable incentive system builds organization-wide trust.

It's hard to let go of the idea that managers should have a role in determining what bonus individual employees receive. Evaluating the performance of the people who report to them is an essential part of every manager's job, arguably the most important. Shouldn't that assessment have an effect on the bonus? And if job evaluations don't affect people's bonus, doesn't that take away a key tool for managers? In our experience, linking job evaluations to bonuses is a bad idea. Manager discretion about bonuses necessarily puts the mechanisms of the incentive system into a black box. Even if employees get feedback on how their own bonus was determined, they won't know about other people's bonuses. Since employees don't know what goes on inside the black box, the natural outcome is rumors, politicking, and hurt feelings. All this is not to say that job evaluations are unimportant. Managers' evaluations are essential to organizational health, but their impact should be on decisions about job promotions, not bonuses.

Tied to Company-Wide Goals

A well-designed bonus system flows from the company goal statement and strategic plan. The connection between the goal statement and the incentive plan should be substantive (the better we do at achieving company goals, the better the incentive payment) and communicative (the incentive plan should be explained using the same words and phases as in the goals statement). This consistent language has the effect of linking the short-horizon goals represented by the incentive system to the long-term perspective represented by the goal statement.

The fundamental driver of the incentive system should be as close to the bottom line as possible. Tying bonus payments to a measure of profitability avoids a number of the troubles that result from bonus programs that go awry. Giving people an incentive to improve quality, for example, may get the company to quality levels that are above what customers need, while driving down production to unacceptable levels. An incentive for improving customer service may end with people spending too much time, or company money, to make people happy. If incentives are targeted at teams of employees, competition may develop between teams for the resources needed to get the biggest bonuses. People from one team may be reluctant to help people in another area if it will hurt their team's performance numbers. Finding the right balance often then leads to complex formulas tying together many factors that no one really understands. Tying the bonus to profitability removes all those problems.

(Even profit has its limitations: an exclusive focus on profits might detract from making decisions that have short-term costs but produce long-term growth. The long-term impact of these short-term decisions, of course, hurts share value, so an ownership stake helps companies balance today's profit with tomorrow's.)

A common objection to this big-picture approach to bonuses is that most people are too distant from the bottom line to feel like they can have any effect on it. A management truism is that people are not motivated to attempt to reach goals when they feel that they can't have any effect on those goals themselves. One way out of this dilemma is to make use of measures other than profit as secondary drivers of the bonus pool. Another is to use mini-games (see the chapter on the Great Game of Business).

But the idea that the bottom line is too remote to be motivational is overblown. Building a link between individual behavior and corporate-level outcomes is challenging, but many companies have done it successfully. Goals and measures that are "closer" to employees will help people make the connection over time, but the belief that most employees cannot see the link between their jobs and company profitability undervalues employees. Employee ownership and a well-designed incentive system both provide employees the motive to understand the connection; the company still needs to provide the means and the opportunity for employees to learn about the connection between their jobs and the company's bottom line. Business literacy and information-sharing systems are the key ingredients. We'll return to these two issues and other ways for your company to support the effectiveness of the incentive program in the final section of this chapter: Integrating the Incentive System.

Building an Incentive System

There are four basic steps to create an incentive program. First, adapt your mission statement or strategic plan into concrete measures to focus on now. Second, create a formula for the pool of money available for the bonus based on those measures. Third, design the way that that pool will be divided up among employees. And last, determine the timing and form of the payouts.

Step 1: Build from the Mission Statement

A mission statement defines what a company is trying to accomplish. Your mission statement should also include a measure of profit. That profit measure is probably your best bet as a primary driver for your incentive program. For some companies, that's all they need for their incentive system. Others will want to reach further into their corporate mission statements or strategic plans to design their incentive plans.

If your company has a strategic plan that spells out the top priorities for the current year, you have a head start on figuring out the two or three concrete measures that you need people to focus on. Sometimes those key measures will address a weakness or a threat; other times they'll be essential steps on a longer path toward the market position your company is aiming for. In most cases, however, the key measures will be the basic elements of successful day-to-day operation: billable hours, gross margin, revenues, defect rates, inventory turns, on-time deliveries, etc. These elements are slightly "closer" to employees than profitability, so it's easier for everyone to see the direct impact that they have on these elements. These top priorities are your secondary drivers.

If your mission statement includes a set of corporate values or ethical standards, those should not be part of the incentive system. Ethical behavior is a minimal standard of professional behavior and not an appropriate subject for reward—paying for good behavior cheapens ethics.

Step 2: Create a Formula for the Bonus Pool

The "bonus pool" is the total amount of money that will be divided up by employees through the incentive program. The bigger the pool, the more money everyone receives, so everyone is motivated to work together to maximize the size of the pool.

Many experts, including Jack Stack of SRC Holdings, argue that the bonus pool should be designed so that it always pays for itself. Bonus pools that are defined as a portion of profits do this automatically. One common formula for a bonus pool is to put a fixed percentage of any profit into the bonus pool after the company reaches a threshold minimum profit. This formula is common because it is simple and elegant, and it works. Companies should, however, engage in a trial-and-error process, probably involving a spreadsheet and a lot of different scenarios, to make sure that the formula makes sense in a wide variety of situations and never creates an excessive bonus pool.

At SRC the primary driver of the bonus pool is simply net income. The company determined that 5% net income is the minimum it needs to generate the working capital it depends on for long-term survival. If net income never breaks that 5% baseline, there won't be a bonus.

In designing the formula, the company also needs to determine if there will be a maximum contribution to the bonus pool. Some companies believe that it's not sustainable to pay a bonus that's too high because of the near-inevitability that the next year's bonus will be a disappointment and a de-motivator. They may also feel that allowing the potential size of the bonus to grow too large may divert people's focus from the long-term health of the company to whatever current-period critical number is driving the bonus, possibly compromising the stability of the company. These companies may set a maximum of the dollar amount of the bonus (a "cap"), or they may gradually decrease the percentage of additional profits that go to employees (a "sliding scale").

We understand the merits of these arguments and have seen that many very successful companies, including SRC, limit the size of the bonus; still, we believe that capping the size of the bonus pool or using a sliding scale weakens the connection between company performance and the incentive program—inevitably, a cap or sliding scale create a less transparent formula. In addition, as long as companies do a good job of business literacy and sharing information, all employees will understand that the rare extraordinary bonus is the result of an extraordinary year and will adjust their own expectations of future bonuses accordingly. As long as performance improvements more than cover the cost of the incentive plan and the formula for the bonus pool is appropriate, we urge companies to avoid caps and sliding scales.

While this corporate-wide pool is a time-proven way to build an incentive program, another approach widely used by successful companies is to integrate both company-wide and local measures into the bonus pool calculation. At SRC, each year's bonus is based on two or three targets, usually including profit and one or two critical weaknesses that need to be addressed. Predictably, progress toward the goals is measured often and communicated in a variety of ways. Meetings are held, notices are sent with paychecks, a ticker tape flashes in the lunch room, and faxes are sent, among other things. At work unit meetings, managers discuss what can be done to meet the targets, and employees share ideas on how to get there.

At Bimba Manufacturing, a 450-person employee-owned manufacturer in Monee, Illinois, quarterly bonuses are paid that can provide up to 10% of an employee's total compensation. Sixty percent is contingent on company-wide profitability, and 40% on specific work group targets. Different departments will have different targets depending on their own contributions to the overall performance of the company. For someone to get a bonus, however, *both* company-wide and local targets must be met. Local targets are set by local managers, working with their employee teams. In addition, there is a separate quarterly bonus of up to $250 per person based on customer service ratings. Targets are tracked weekly, and for each week the target is met, $20 is added to the bonus. The bonus system is one of the 16 sessions taught in new-hire orientation, and ongoing progress is tracked in a variety of ways, including the newsletter, annual meetings, team meetings, posting of results, one-on-one conversations, and local meetings. Weekly customer service data flow from managers to individual work units. The bonus system is not static, however. It can and has changed over time as new problems emerged and existing ones were solved.

One of the common themes from Bimba and SRC is that the short-term reward system is built around *both* corporate and local goals. Especially in a larger company, employees may not think that what they and their group do makes much difference to how the company performs. While it can be dispiriting to people not to get a bonus because the company does poorly while their unit performs very well, in the long term, no individual group will succeed unless the company succeeds. Paying out based on both measures provides people with an effective "line of sight" between what they do and what they get. Moreover, it fosters cooperation and focus on corporate goals. The tension between rewarding for corporate-level performance and local performance has no right answer, but we believe that companies more often err on the side of giving too much weight to local issues.

Step 3: Create an Allocation Formula

Once you have a pool of bonus money, the next step is to decide who gets how much of the pool. Some companies use very simple formulas, such as relative pay: the more you earn in W-2 compensation, the bigger your bonus. The principle behind this strategy is that compensation is a good gauge of the contribution each individual makes to the company, and therefore to the bonus.

Other companies believe that different principles apply to compensation and bonus: the market for labor creates competition, but teamwork determines the level of company success. Therefore, the principles for allocating wages should be different than for allocating bonuses. These companies use a variety of formulas: the simplest is a "solidarity approach," where everyone gets the same bonus, "from the president to the janitor," as Don Madison, the former President of Marland Mold in Pittsfield, Massachusetts, says. Other companies use different non-wage formulas, based on years of service, for example. For the monthly bonus program at the Spicer Axle Division of Dana Industries, the bonus is allocated to people in proportion to the number of hours they worked during that month.

Part of the allocation formula is determining who is eligible for a bonus. In *Ideas Are Free*, Alan Robinson and Dean Schroeder make an eloquent case that an effective way to generate ideas is to use idea submission as a criteria for bonus eligibility. It doesn't matter whether an employee's ideas are good or not—the process of evaluating the ideas and the inherent desire we all have to make a difference in our worlds provide all the incentive we need to improve our ideas over time. For the bonus pool, make every employee who submits a minimum number of ideas eligible for the bonus—once people start submitting ideas and seeing them implemented, the quality of the ideas will take care of itself.

One company that prefers to remain anonymous has a simple formula for the bonus pool (a flat percentage of profit, starting at the first dollar) and a creative allocation formula. Half of the pool is allocated based on seniority, where there is both a floor and a ceiling on the number of seniority points an employee can accumulate. The other portion of the pool is proportional to each employee's W-2 compensation adjusted to reflect the employee's performance review and the number of process improvements that employee submitted using the company's system.

At Keller-Schroder, a technology consulting firm (and not related to Dean Schroeder), there is an "indexed performance bonus." All employees have a target bonus assigned to them based on their expected contributions to the company. The actual bonus paid out is based on earnings versus the budget target. If the excess is 10% over target, everyone's target bonus goes up 10%; if earnings beat target by 20%, then the increment is 20%. In a down year, everyone shares in the pain in similar proportions.

One principle for the allocation formula and the bonus pool formula is simplicity. Some incentive programs are so carefully tweaked to adjust to all foreseeable scenarios that they end up a Byzantine maze of complex formulas, caps, floors, conditions, and obscure ratios. Companies with such complicated formulas may as well tell employees that bonuses will be determined by a random number generator: they'll never feel that they understand how the bonus number was determined or what impact they could possibly have on it. Do not underestimate the value of being able to explain your bonus system in one sentence.

Step 4: Determine the Timing and Form of the Payout

The arguments for less frequent bonus payments are persuasive: you never want the bonus payout to take cash that the company is going to need later, and you don't want to force the accounting people to spend so much time generating numbers to calculate bonuses that they don't have time for other tasks.

On the other hand, the arguments for more frequent payouts are persuasive as well. People won't have much of a reason to focus on results until they see that the bonus is within reach.

A common approach to solving this problem is to pay out quarterly in increasing increments (a maximum of 10% of the goal in the first quarter, 20% in the second, 30% in the third, and 40% in the fourth). If the target is not met in a quarter, the remaining amount can be rolled forward to the next quarter, so, conceivably, the company could fail to meet all its goals in the first three quarters and then pay out 100% of target in the last quarter. This rolling program avoids the twin traps of not giving people anything soon enough to keep them interested but not losing their interest by meeting the maximum payout early in the year.

Another approach, used with great success by Reflexite Corporation, is to pay a monthly bonus. Reflexite calls it an "owners' bonus," and part of the strength of its program lies in the explicit connection Reflexite makes between the incentive program and two other components of ownership management: business literacy and shared financial information. When a Reflexite employee owner receives an owner's bonus check, the check comes with a simplified five-line financial statement for the month. The operating profit (the "bottom line" on the simplified statement) for the month is multiplied by a fixed percentage that goes into the bonus pool. Each employee's share of the bonus pool is also clearly marked—it's printed on the check.

It's easier for companies to increase the frequency of bonus payments if the size of the payments is small relative to pay. Any retroactive accounting changes or unexpected future demands on cash will be less affected by the bonus payments, and many companies find that frequent bonus payments increase their informational value and actually increase motivation to the extent that people see the bonus as an indicator of the increasing value of the company they own.

Pool Covers, a small 100% ESOP-owned company in Fairfield, California, that installs and maintains swimming pool covers, uses a completely different approach to the bonus. In its "bucket system," targets are set to certain critical numbers; when they are reached, employees get a cash bonus. The advantage of a bucket system is that it eliminates waiting until the end of the period—it is a "pay as you go" incentive system. The bucket system, however, is not the best approach for companies where bonus payments may turn out to be needed later.

So far, the form of the incentive payout has been cash, but there is no reason it needs to be. Companies can set up programs that pay out in the form of stock options or restricted shares. They can also pay in cash, where the amount of payout is linked to the value of a share of stock, such as stock appreciation rights or phantom stock.

Still another approach with regard to timing of payouts focuses on the medium term. ATA Engineering of San Diego, California, has an ESOP to provide an incentive in the long term and a cash bonus for the short term. ATA Engineering decided that it needed to fill in the gap between those programs and created a system of stock options. All employees participate annually so employees have "waves" of options: they always look toward the five- to ten-year time horizon over which their options will come into the money.

Integrating the Incentive Program

Any incentive plan, even your company's hypothetical ideal one, will fail miserably unless it fits in with everything else your company does: it should reinforce the importance of the information your company shares, reflect the same priorities as your strategic plan, reward the same behavior as job evaluations, and the language of the bonus should be part of ongoing corporate communications. Too many companies develop a wonderful incentive plan and then excitedly introduce it, only to realize that they should have taken more time to start integrating the plan into the company. Here are some ways to make that integration happen.

Business Literacy

Business literacy shows people how their role fits into the overall success of the company. Creating widespread business literacy takes work, but it's essential not only to the effectiveness of the incentive program but to people's ability to understand how they relate to the company and its success. The NCEO has extensive resources on business literacy, so suffice it to say that you can build business literacy starting from simple concepts like critical numbers. Critical numbers will ideally be the drivers in your incentive formula. From there you can build to key concepts (revenue versus profit, risk and reward, cash versus profit, investment versus expense) and more detail about your own business model and financial statements. Eventually, you will want people to understand something about stock valuation, your company's strategic plan, and opportunity costs.

An even more basic level of business literacy that is surprisingly neglected is education about the mechanics of the incentive plan itself. Equity compensation plans such as stock options or stock appreciation rights are often the form in which incentive plans make their payouts, but the authors of the NCEO's current practices survey on equity compensation issues observe that "the low prevalence of all types of communication and education is remarkable." Over half (52%) of companies did not have *any* form of ongoing communication about their stock option programs and almost a quarter (23%) did not communicate about their plans to employees at the time of grant. The most common communications technique was a letter from senior management, followed by individual meetings between employees and their supervisors and group meetings with human resources.

Integrate with Your Information Systems

Another way to help people see the connections between themselves, overall profitability, and the incentive payout is through sharing information. Suppose I work in the warehouse and every week I see a chart telling me how much inventory we have on hand and how much it's increasing or decreasing. Every week my supervisor tells me how much more the company spent on materials and what impact that has on cash flow. I may only have an impact on a small portion of the items in inventory, but if I propose an operational improvement that's implemented, I may see the impact of my idea in the next week's cash flow statement. Suddenly, I'm not just managing widget levels—I'm playing the great game of business, and I'm helping my team win.

Link to Ownership

Some companies believe that the most effective bonus is explicitly tied to ownership, like Reflexite Corporation's Owners' Bonus. Making short-term rewards in the form of an equity-linked security (like phantom stock or stock appreciation rights) or dividends on company stock can give people a greater appreciation for their stock holdings. Dividends reward the people who have stayed the longest and thus have accumulated larger accounts, but they can also be dispiriting for newer employees with few shares in their accounts—they'll only see nominal dividend amounts in the early years even though they have worked very hard to help the company grow. Rather than use actual dividends, most companies are well served by using the language of ownership in their incentive programs and constantly reminding people of the link between profitability and share value.

Be Ready Not to Pay

So what happens when you come close but don't quite make the bonus? There is no easy answer to this question, but there is a right answer. Don't pay. Jack Stack has been in this position—he has seen bonus targets missed by 0.01%. He writes "Once you start changing the rules of the game, you step onto a slippery slope, and it is hard to go back." If the point of employee ownership is to treat people like entrepreneurs, then reality matters, and a missed target is a missed target. If a manager decides to intervene and pay the bonus anyway, Stack argues, then we are no longer playing the great game of business in the marketplace; we're playing with our manager, who decides whether we win or lose. Changing the rules mid-game shifts the focus from external measures to internal organizational dynamics—just where you don't want them.

One helpful way to frame this issue is to think about the short-term versus long-term effect of not paying the bonus. In the short term, everyone will be disappointed, maybe angry. In the longer term, you have increased the credibility of the incentive program, the importance of shared financial information, the impact of business literacy, and, if your company is employee owned, made ownership real. If people experience the downside of ownership in downtimes, that makes them responsible for the upside in good times—the future impact of not paying the bonus is to make people believe in their role as entrepreneurs.

Cultivate the Language of the Bonus

In companies with effective plans, people talk business. They're engaged in problem solving, in projecting performance, in capturing opportunities. For them to have these conversations, they need a shared language and shared goals. An incentive program provides both. People know what the company is trying to accomplish *right now*. They understand the definition and measurement of that goal, and they know what needs to happen to reach that goal. The bonus program provides a ready-to-use ice breaker for any person in your company to approach any other person to brainstorm or test out ideas to promote company performance.

It's More Than Money

People want to make a difference. They want to be creative, have their ideas tested, and see the impact they can have. An incentive system, when it's working properly, serves just that function: it shows people a concrete measure of the value of their ideas. Dollars are a great yardstick, and having a cash bonus makes it obvious that the company is serious about valuing employee input. When business-literate employees are constantly informed about the key measures of corporate health, they can track the impact that they and their colleagues are having on the company. And when those employees see their impact reflected the annual stock valuation, you have closed the loop. People take responsibility for company success because they are thinking like owners.

A counterintuitive implication is that short-term money is not necessarily the most important motivator in an incentive system. When you divide up your total compensation budget, don't overlook the potential benefits of a modest amount for short-term incentives.

Design the Incentive Participatively

Before you roll out a new ownership-friendly incentive system, you should consider involving employees in its design. Rather than simply adopt an incentive program, management at Zandex Health Care Corporation circulated it in draft form. All 1,000 employees at the company had an opportunity to comment, with ongoing feedback continuing until a broadly supported program was developed.

Another successful participative approach is to create cross-sectional committees with the task of building or modifying an incentive program. Company leaders should carefully frame the role for the committee and reserve the right to overrule it if necessary to ensure that the resulting plan is legal, practical, and supports the company mission statement. The committee should understand that the system needs to meet the criteria in this chapter: for example, the plan should be formula driven, should pay for itself, and should use the language of ownership. The committee can help with the communication around the incentive program: members will be able to craft language that speaks better to the work force than senior management would be able to.

Still, the real advantage of using a participative design process for your incentive program is greater than that. The purpose of a formula-driven incentive system is to explode the black box of decision making and make the incentive system transparent. Having employees help design the incentive takes the principle of transparency to an even deeper level and results in the system being "born" with a built-in level of credibility that's impossible in a management- or consultant-designed system.

In fact, this reflects a deeper principle. Ginny Vanderslice, an employee ownership consultant at Praxis Consulting Group, has long advocated the idea that employee participation, when done right, results not only in better decisions, but faster implementation of those decisions. An employee committee often comes up with solutions that fit more comfortably with the organization's culture, and the natural feeling of the decision reduces resistance to change. She has repeatedly observed that for her clients, faster and more effective implementation more than makes up for the extra time required in the design stage of a participative process.

Conclusion

Like anything else in business, incentive systems take a lot of work and, unless you are very lucky, a lot of tweaking to get right. Even if you set up a system that works well at first, it may work less well over time as people and business conditions change. So be ready to do more tweaking as needed. Finally, remember that while a perfect system probably does not exist for your company, don't let the insistence on perfection stop you from implementing a program that, while imperfect, is nonetheless an improvement.

CHAPTER 3

Creating Ownership Thinking with Incentive Pay

Brad Hams

This chapter[1] is dedicated to the subject of creating effective incentive plans and how to engage employees in funding those plans. Creating effective incentive plans is not an easy task, but by focusing on what makes people think and act like owners, it is one that companies can accomplish.

The model in figure 3.1 represents the four components of what I call ownership thinking: The Right People, The Right Education, The Right Measures, and The Right Incentives. "The Right Incentives" is actually the last component of the Ownership Thinking Model, but it tends to be the topic that both employees and management want to hear about first. I suppose there are two reasons for this. The first is because it's the WIIFM (What's In It For Me) component. Second, many, if not most, incentive plans out there don't work very well, and so there is a good deal of frustration (and therefore cynicism) about them among both employees and employers. Incentive plans need to be financially meaningful to employees but at the same time be self-funding. If an incentive plan does not pay for itself, then you've simply created a new expense, one that is more entitlement than inducement. Educating employees about why a plan has to strike this balance is essential.

---

1. "Ownership Thinking" is a trademarked term created by Brad Hams, president of Ownership Thinking, Inc. In this chapter, the term "ownership thinking" is also used in a generic sense and not capitalized. This chapter is adapted from a forthcoming book by Brad Hams on the subject, *Eradicate Entitlement: How to Create an Organization of Employees Who Think and Act Like Owners.*

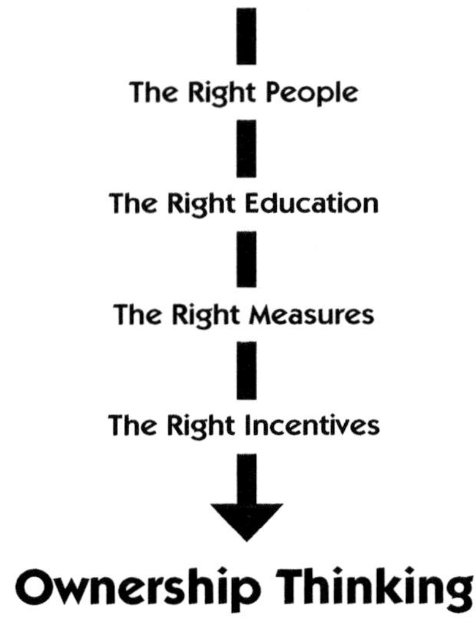

Figure 3.1. The ownership thinking model

This point about an incentive plan not being an expense is a fundamentally important one. I have found that many, if not most, business owners and leaders look at incentives as if they were a budgeted expense, so clearly there might not be a lot of enthusiasm about creating one. I suggest you look at it this way instead: by implementing an ownership thinking way of doing business, your profitability will increase from X to Y, and quite often Y will be substantially greater than X. The organization now has additional profit dollars that are represented by the gap between X and Y, and the bonus (I will use the terms bonus and incentive plan interchangeably) will be a portion of that gap. Given this, the bonus is not only self-funded, but it will also drive the profitability of the organization higher, even after the bonus payout is made. *Everyone* must understand this simple premise: the incentive plan is meant to improve the financial performance of the company and to shape employee behavior accordingly. Incentives should never be paid if financial performance does not warrant them.

In this chapter, I will outline elements of poorly designed incentive plans, elements of well designed plans, and how to design a successful plan.

Elements of Poorly Designed Incentive Plans

It was pretty clear to me before starting my practice that most incentive plans I'd seen did not work, and, in fact, many actually damaged the organization. So when I started doing this work back in the mid-1990s, I decided to do a little research on what companies typically did wrong in the design of their incentive plans. I found the following to be common mistakes:

1. The plans created separate fiefdoms.
2. They were discretionary.
3. Employees felt that (true or not) the goals were unrealistic or unattainable.
4. The payout opportunity was too small, so there was no perceived value.
5. The goals of the plan were not communicated, so employees could not see the connection between the work they did and the bonuses they received.
6. The goals of the plan would change during the communicated time frame of the plan.

1. Separate Fiefdoms

When business owners or leaders set out to create an incentive plan, I think many of them start with the underlying idea that if they just create the right plan, it will manage their people. With this in mind, they may say to themselves "if this department or individual is required to do X, Y, and Z, then I will create an incentive plan tied to their performance of X, Y, and Z." More often than not, X, Y, and Z are not financially quantifiable. They will then go through the same exercise with the other departments or individuals throughout the organization. As you might imagine, the result is a ridiculously complex set of incentives that is universally not understood (and therefore not trusted) by employees and is a nightmare to administer. Most important, however, they have now created a situation where each department or individual is being motivated to look out for their own best interest rather than the best interest of the organization as a whole. As a result, they may actually sabotage another area of the company in order to ensure they meet their goals and receive their bonus.

For example, I was working with a $70 million construction company some time back that was significantly underperforming financially. The company had multiple incentive plans in place, as I was describing, and I noted that one region was consistently receiving bonuses while the others were not. I discovered that this region manager had been hoarding all of the best equipment (even equipment he was not using at the moment) and all of the best people to ensure he met his goals. Obviously, the rest of the company was suffering from these actions.

Another potential outcome of multiple plans like this is that there is no assurance the company will be profitable, even if some departments or individuals are receiving a bonus. Finally, it is virtually impossible to create multiple plans and remain objective. If managers are to determine who will be receiving bonuses and who will not, they will quite often give them to the people they simply like the best. This, of course, raises questions of fairness and will likely damage morale.

I'm not including the sales department in the analysis above. I do think it must be treated differently (in most cases), and, in fact, the marketplace often demands this. Commissions are fine as long as they are designed properly, meaning they may not be only about revenue. I've always considered the role of a salesperson to be a "champion of margin." In other words, it's not just about bringing revenue to the table, but about *profitable revenue*. The absolute worst scenario I encounter is when a salesperson is commissioned on revenue and has the ability to negotiate or manipulate pricing. You are just asking for reduced margins in this case. Given this, I suggest you set up one of the following: (1) salespeople are commissioned on revenue, and pricing is engraved in stone, or (2) salespeople can negotiate pricing and are commissioned on margin. If you choose the latter, it's critical that you teach them everything they need to know about margins and have a sliding commission scale that allows them to do better if they are bringing higher-margin sales to the table. The remaining question, then, is whether they will also participate in the broad-based plan. Generally, I would say yes, because I want them to be thinking about overall company performance, not simply their little world of sales.

When I discuss distribution methods later in the chapter, I will touch on this again.

2. Discretionary Bonuses

Your company has had a pretty good year, and there is a little money left in the checking account at year end. And so, probably at Christmas time, you hand out checks to everyone. Yea! This might make you feel good (although it is somewhat paternalistic), and it will probably make your employees feel good for the moment, but all you've really given them is a gift. Remember, the purpose of an incentive plan is to shape employee behavior toward improving the financial performance of the company. The gift you gave them is not tied to behavior and therefore will not change behavior until, perhaps, employees don't get the gift! Once again, you have created an entitlement.

3. Getting Employees to Buy In to Practical Goals

An office furniture distributor I was working with had just come off a very tough year (roughly $9 million in revenue and a $395,000 loss). After we had worked with the leadership team to identify their key performance indicators and done some work with both leadership and employees to determine where money had been falling through the cracks, it was determined that for the upcoming year, a budget of $11 million in revenue and a profit of $550,000 (5%) was doable as a stretch goal. The employees bought into this stretch goal because they were shown where the cracks were and had been a part of the planning to seal them up. Here are a few of them:

- Poor labor efficiency due to lack of job costing
- Sales team was focused on revenue rather than margin, and had been discounting
- A lack of emphasis on service sales (rather than product sales), which were generally more profitable
- Excessive punch list items requiring follow-up work without the ability to invoice

- Errors in order entry: finish, fabric, pricing, etc.
- Installation damage and concealed damage on receipt of product
- Excessive non-billable overtime
- High average collection days
- Small tool loss and damage

Imagine if none of this work had been done with the leadership or employees, and the owner of the company had simply come up with this budget by himself, in a vacuum. As an employee, how would you feel about that budget, knowing that you had just come off a loss year? Of course you wouldn't buy into it, and most likely you would simply think the owner was dreaming (or out of his mind). My point is that because employees were actively involved in identifying the money falling through the cracks, and agreed that these areas could indeed be improved upon using ownership thinking tools, they bought into this stretch goal. This company actually exceeded the stretch goal in its first year of practicing ownership thinking. The lesson is, it is not necessarily whether the budget is realistic or not that's important, but rather if your employees believe in the goals they set for themselves.

4. No Perceived Value

A bonus opportunity of $10 a year is probably not going to motivate people (in fact it might irritate them). A bonus opportunity of 10% of their salary is something quite different. In other words, the bonus opportunity (at a stretch goal) should be enough to get people's attention. Having said this, it must always be clear that the bonus will be self-funded. I will clarify this when we get to plan design a bit later in this chapter.

5. Goals Are Not Communicated

One of the biggest problems with the majority of incentive plans is that there is a very weak link (or no link at all) between the work that employees are doing and the bonuses they are receiving (or not). If the goal of the plan is to shape behavior, then it is critical that employees have a clear understanding of the goals that have been set for the plan. If the plan is based on profit before tax (PBT), they must know what the threshold is, what the stretch goal is, what the payout opportunity is after the threshold, etc. Just as important, they must know what key performance indicators (KPIs) must be focused on to find the money to fund the plan, and they must have the tools and information to become active participants in driving those KPIs. If this link is not clearly made, and if employees are not active participants, then the plan will (once again) become an entitlement plan.

6. Changing the Plan During the Communicated Time Period

I generally suggest that incentive plans be tied to projected annual profit performance. Further, I suggest that they be divided into quarterly opportunities, a good practice that makes the incentive more immediate and flexible. Once designed, the plan should be communicated to your employees along with key areas of focus to ensure the plan will be funded. I suggest that you reevaluate your incentive plan every year as you go through your budgeting process, and it is likely that you will tweak it from year to year. The design may stay fundamentally the same, but the numbers will change based on revenue growth, improvements in operational efficiencies, changes in product or client strategy, etc. When you introduce the plan each year, reiterate to employees that this is the plan for the upcoming year but there is no guarantee that it will remain unchanged for subsequent years. Having said this, I strongly advise you not to mess with the plan during the year for which it has been designed.

I've seen two different scenarios. In the first, the organization comes out of the gate very strong, and, for example, may have two great quarters with substantial bonus payouts. The owners may become anxious about the size of the bonus payouts (even though the plan is self-funded) and decide to change the targets for the remainder of the year. Obviously, the credibility of the plan will be shot. Your employees will not forget this, either, and it may take several years before they regain trust in the incentive plan (or in you). In the second scenario, the company comes up a little short on its goals. The owners want to be nice, however, and since everyone has been so "busy," they decide to pay out a bonus anyway. The credibility of this plan has been shot, too. Moreover, the message sent to your employees is that it doesn't really matter if they hit the goals or not. Once again, you have an entitlement plan.

Elements of Well-Designed Incentive Plans

Below are the elements of well-designed plans:

1. They are self-funding, and they ensure financial and value enhancements to the business.
2. They have perceived value.
3. They have shared targets.
4. The goals are understandable.
5. The goals are attainable (though not a "gimme").
6. They clearly align employee behavior to business objectives.

1. Self-Funding, and Driving Organizational Performance

From a financial perspective, the most important aspect of an incentive plan is that it pays for itself and adds value to the organization. If you base your plan on PBT, you must first determine a minimum acceptable threshold of PBT before which no bonus will be paid. A common pushback I get from employees on this is: "If the bonus is based on profit, and all expenses are covered, why not begin paying out a bonus from dollar one of profit?" First, all expenses have not been covered if the bonus is based on PBT. The expense that has not been addressed is, of course, the big T (tax). This is no small chunk of change, either, and you should inform your employees that businesses typically pay 40% of profit in taxes. There are other organizational needs that must be considered beyond simply expenses, however. Businesses need capital for investments or improvements (such as equipment, which is capitalized rather than expensed), debt retirement, and, of course, return on investment for the shareholders. By addressing all of these needs, you can arrive at a minimum threshold of profit that will ensure the company has the capital it needs to operate effectively and meet its growth objectives before any bonus considerations are made. The percentage share beyond this threshold should then allow for the organization to retain a reasonable level of profit after bonuses are distributed.

2. Perceived Value

As I mentioned in the fourth element of poorly designed plans, an annual bonus opportunity of $10 is not going to do much to motivate your employees. I have found that a bonus opportunity of 8% to 12% of wages will really get employees' attention. There is nothing particularly scientific about that range; it is just based on my experience. The question then becomes how to come up with a bonus opportunity in this range and still ensure that the plan meets your objectives. The steps I suggest are as follows:

- Determine your threshold as described above.
- Determine a realistic stretch goal. This number is not just snatched out of the air. It should be based on historical performance, plus additional profit expectations from your focus on the KPIs that have been identified and the "Rapid Improvement Plans" that will be put into place to drive them. Note that the bonus pool will be funded once the threshold has been surpassed (or is trending to be surpassed), and the stretch goal is something greater.
- Identify the budgeted payroll dollars for the year in question (compensation only, no taxes, commissions, or benefits).

Once these have been identified, you can identify a percentage of profit to share with your employees that will meet the 8% to 12% payout criterion once the stretch goal has been achieved. As an example, if the minimum threshold is $500,000 and the stretch goal is $800,000, the gap between these is $300,000. If the payroll budget is $1.2 million, and it is your goal to have a 10% bonus opportunity at the stretch goal, then the percentage of profit after meeting the threshold that should go toward the bonus pool is 40%. Forty percent of $300,000 is $120,000, or 10% of the total payroll (see table 3.1).

Table 3.1. Bonus Pool Calculation

PBT after payout	PBT	Incentive pool (40%)
$500,000	$500,000	$0
$530,000	$550,000	$20,000
$560,000	$600,000	$40,000
$590,000	$650,000	$60,000
$620,000	$700,000	$80,000
$650,000	$750,000	$100,000
$680,000	**$800,000**	**$120,000**
$710,000	$850,000	$140,000
$740,000	$900,000	$160,000
$770,000	$950,000	$180,000
$800,000	$1,000,000	$200,000

Though the bonus payout objective is 8% to 12% of wages if the stretch goal is reached, this may not be realistic in every situation. I sometimes work with companies that have been marginally profitable for some time (due to performance rather than industry limitations), and to draft a plan that assumes they will move from a break-even or loss position to a 5% or 10% profit in year one is probably unrealistic. In this situation, the bonus opportunity at the stretch goal may be something significantly less than 8% to 12%, perhaps 3% or 4%. More often than not, these companies have not been paying bonuses (shame on them if they have), and so anything is better than nothing. By practicing ownership thinking, they should be able to get their profitability up to a level that will allow for a more interesting bonus opportunity after a couple of years.

3. Shared Targets

As I mentioned in my discussion of "separate fiefdoms" above, there are several reasons to avoid creating an incentive plan that is tied to departmental or individual goals. The ultimate objective should always be to meet or exceed the profitability goal of the organization. This is not to say that bonuses will be distributed equally to all employees (I will discuss distribution methods later in the chapter), but simply that the bonus *pool* will be based on the performance of the company versus the performance of any one department or individual. Everyone in the organization should be focused on this objective.

4. Understandable Goals

One of the reasons I suggest PBT as the driver of your incentive is that it is fairly easy to understand. It is simply the company's revenue, less its expenses. Another reason is that every employee in the organization can impact PBT in one way or another (they simply need to be taught how). I've seen companies base their incentive plans on EBITDA, for example, which is Earnings Before Interest, Taxes, Depreciation, and Amortization. Others have based theirs on EVA (Economic Value Added), or ROC (Return On Capital). In each of these cases, employees' eyes will likely glaze over when the plan is communicated to them. Once again, if they do not understand what drives the plan, it will have little or no impact on their behavior. In addition, they will probably not trust it.

5. Achievable Goals

Employees must believe that the goals are achievable, though it should be clear that improved financial performance is required to fund the plan. As I mentioned in my previous comments about unrealistic goals, the issue is quite often not whether the goals are achievable as much as ensuring that employees are receiving all of the information and tools they need to recognize and find the money that has been "falling through the cracks." Employees will often be skeptical of this at the outset, but seeing is believing, and they will gain enthusiasm as they see improvements and their contributions toward those improvements. I typically acknowledge the skepticism that people have at the beginning (after all, many organizations have taught their employees that there is a lack of follow-through on initiatives), but at the same time I make it clear that they must participate.

6. Clearly Align Employee Behavior to Business Objectives

The fundamental premise of ownership thinking is to create cultures of employees who think and act like owners about creating wealth. If the desired result of your incentive plan is to increase the profitability of your organization, then the plan must be tied to the profitability of the organization. This, frankly, is the simple part. The more difficult part is providing the training and creating the structures for information sharing and employee involvement that can help them find the ways to meet the targets. These issues will be discussed in my book and are also discussed in other NCEO publications, particularly *The Ownership Edge.*

Designing Your Plan

Now that you are familiar with the elements of poorly designed incentive plans compared to well-designed incentive plans, the design elements should make a good deal of sense to you. There are 10 questions you must answer in order to design your plan:

1. What is the key indicator that will drive the plan (or in a few cases, two key indicators)?
2. Who will participate?
3. What is our threshold?
4. What is our stretch goal?
5. What is our total payroll? Number of employees?
6. What is our percentage share (to get to 10%)?
7. Cap or no cap? If yes, what is it?
8. What is our distribution method?
9. Should the plan be quarterly, annual, or something else?
10. Should there be a separate management pool?

1. What Is the Key Indicator That Will Drive the Plan?

Almost all of the plans we design are tied to profit before tax. Again, this is the score that your employees can impact (most cannot impact tax). On rare occasions, I suggest that you have a second key indicator that drives cash flow. For example, one of our clients, a roughly $10 million company, had a history of collection problems. A particularly uncomfortable situation to be in is when you have to pay out a bonus because the company met its profitability goal, but there is no cash to pay it. So what do you do? Borrow money to pay the bonus? Ouch. For this company, then, the bonus was tied to PBT, but there was a caveat tied to AR. If the company was at 45 average collection days or less at the date of bonus distribution, then the entire bonus was paid. From 45 to 50, the payout was 50%, and if they were 50 days or more, there was no payout.

2. Who Will Participate?

In nearly every case, I strongly advise my clients that everyone should participate in the incentive plan, which is why I call them "broad-based plans." This is not to say that the bonus pool is equally distributed, but simply that everyone participates. Keep this in mind: everyone can contribute to the financial performance of the company, and everyone can sabotage it. As I said before, we want to create organizations of excellence, not pockets of excellence.

If you determine that the plan will be broad-based, then the question is no longer "who participates," but rather "how do they participate?" I will answer this question a little later on in my discussion of distribution methods and separate management pools.

On rare occasions I have come across an organization where it didn't necessarily make sense to include everyone in the incentive plan. Typically, it is a company that exhibits these characteristics:

- There are several distinct levels within the organization, i.e., laborers to executives and everything in between.
- The laborers are somewhat transient, and/or the business is highly seasonal.
- The incentive for laborers is overtime.

Another circumstance that might call for the exclusion of some employees is a union shop. Unions are quite often not very receptive to any type of pay-for-performance plan, and so they may be difficult to sell on the idea. It's a pity, because I've always believed that what unions should be working toward for their members are (a) competitive wages, (b) a safe environment, and (c) security. From my experience, there is no better way to achieve these things for employees than by practicing ownership thinking. If you want to include your union, I suggest that you approach it from this angle. If you can sell the union on the idea, then it becomes quite easy to implement with the support of the union. I worked with a division of Alcoa once that was able to engage its union, and the outcome was fascinating. Not only was there a tremendous amount of buy-in and performance enhancements (both operationally and financially), but union member grievances virtually disappeared.

3. What Is Our Threshold?

As previously mentioned, every organization will have financial needs (capital needs) beyond just its expenses. These will typically include, but not necessarily be limited to, ROI for shareholders, debt retirement, and capital for improvements or investments. Depending on the structure of your business, you must consider tax as well (assuming the bonus is based on PBT). Your threshold is simply the amount of profit required to address these financial needs of the company. No bonus will be paid until the company is trending to meet this threshold. I'll explain how to calculate this a bit later.

4. What Is Our Stretch Goal?

This number can be determined by examining the following:

- What has the historical performance of the company been?
- What does our budget look like for the coming year?
- What kind of money do we think has been falling through the cracks here?

5. What Is Our Total Payroll? Number of Employees?

You will need the total payroll number (wages only, excluding taxes, benefits, bonuses, and commissions) to help determine what percentage of PBT after your threshold will be going into the bonus pool. Again, a bonus pool that is 8% to 12% of total wages at your stretch goal is ideal but not always realistic. By playing around with the percentage share, you can determine what would be necessary to get you to this number. I rarely suggest a number higher than 40%, but I occasionally build a plan with a 50% share.

The total number of employees (or full-time equivalents) is only needed if you will be distributing the plan equally. You will need it to create the spread sheet showing the payout schedule at different levels of profitability (see table 3.2).

6. What Is the Percentage Share?

Again, this is the percentage of profit after the minimum threshold that will be funding the bonus plan. I have already discussed this in some detail, but there is one more design element that you may want to consider. If you have an organization that has been marginally profitable in previous years, yet you wish to have a plan that would offer some payout even at a level that does not meet your long-term goals (or industry standards, perhaps), you may want to create a plan with escalating payouts. For example, 20% of PBT after a minimum threshold of X will go to the bonus pool, 30% of PBT after exceeding milestone Y will go to the bonus pool, and 40% of PBT after exceeding milestone Z.

7. Should the Plan Have a Cap, and If So, What Should It Be?

By capping the plan, I simply mean identifying a maximum bonus payout opportunity. For example, an organization may decide to cap the bonus at 15% of total wages. Once this payout has been achieved, any further profit will not allow for a contribution to the plan. I generally do not suggest doing this. As you might expect, if the maximum payout has been achieved, some steam may come out of the plan. Keep in mind that the plan is self-funding, and that by following the guidelines and principles outlined in this book, your employees will be active participants in funding the plan. Having said all this, I do suggest capping the plan in a few situations and have noted them below.

Table 3.2. Equal Distribution of Ownership Pool

PBT	Incentive pool	Q1 (50% held)	Q2 (50% held)	Q3 (50% held)	Q4 total adjusted	Total	× 75 employees
$900,000	$0	$0	$0	$0	$0	$0	$0
$1,000,000	$40,000	$67	$67	$67	$333	$533	$40,000
$1,100,000	$80,000	$133	$133	$133	$667	$1,067	$80,000
$1,200,000	$120,000	$200	$200	$200	$1,000	$1,600	$120,000
$1,300,000	$160,000	$267	$267	$267	$1,333	$2,133	$160,000
$1,400,000	$200,000	$333	$333	$333	$1,667	$2,667	$200,000
$1,500,000	**$240,000**	**$400**	**$400**	**$400**	**$2,000**	**$3,200**	**$240,000**
$1,600,000	$280,000	$467	$467	$467	$2,333	$3,733	$280,000
$1,700,000	$320,000	$533	$533	$533	$2,667	$4,267	$320,000
$1,800,000	$360,000	$600	$600	$600	$3,000	$4,800	$360,000
$1,900,000	$400,000	$667	$667	$667	$3,333	$5,333	$400,000

- In companies with an ESOP or some other form of broad-based equity sharing plan, I will usually suggest capping the incentive plan. My reasoning is that in these organizations, PBT is no longer the "score at the end of the game." The end game is now stock value. These organizations must focus more on retained earnings and building a strong balance sheet toward this end. In addition, many ESOPs are leveraged (meaning they took on debt to make the transaction), and so additional cash is needed to retire the debt.
- I generally suggest capping the plan in non-profit organizations. It may seem counterintuitive, but you can indeed have a bonus plan in non-profits, although the driver will not be called profit, but something like net operating income or excess income. The reason for capping the plan is that if the organization is audited and it is deemed that organization members are receiving "unreasonable compensation," the organization can lose its non-profit status.
- I sometimes suggest capping a plan in industries that have wild swings in profitability, particularly if those swings are clearly tied to market conditions (such as interest rates).

In any case, it's not a bad idea to write a caveat into your plan that allows for management to adjust the payout if something outside of normal operations creates an inordinately high payout situation. Examples may be the sale of a significant asset or unexpected income from investments.

If you do decide to cap your plan for one of the reasons noted here, the final question is "what should that cap be?" I don't have a formula to offer. I simply suggest that the number be one that will ensure that the short- and long-term goals of the company will be met. If you have a non-profit, or some other organizational structure where you have any doubts about the legality of your plan, then it is always wise to consult a lawyer with some expertise in that area. In most metropolitan areas, there will also be some sort of employer assistance organization that can be used as a resource (in Denver, for example, there is an organization called the Mountain States Employers Council).

8. What Will Your Distribution Method Be?

This is often the biggest discussion point of an incentive plan. Now that we have identified the pool of money that may be available to employees, how will it be distributed to them? I will offer three alternatives, and one of them will fit most organizations' needs or situation.

The first distribution method, and perhaps the most common, is distribution based on wages. In other words, the individual employee's compensation, divided by the total wages of the company, will determine the payout of that individual. With this method, every employee receives a bonus payout that is the same percentage of his or her salary. Given this, employees with higher salaries will receive a larger bonus (in terms of dollars). Most employees will accept this as an equitable method of distribution, understanding that the people with higher salaries typically have more responsibility, more experience, and are typically salaried rather than hourly and therefore exempt from overtime pay.

The second method is simply equal distribution of the bonus pool among all employees, regardless of their position or compensation. Adjustments may be made for those who work less than a standard 40-hour work week or work on a seasonal basis. This is very easy to administer, since the bonus pool is simply divided by the number of employees and distributed accordingly. It also sends a very powerful message (we're all in this together), which is perhaps why these companies statistically (from our experience) perform better. This statistic is not entirely reliable, however, due to the fact that the majority of companies that share equally are smaller, flatter (meaning few levels of management) companies. The larger and more complex a company, the less likely it is to choose this method.

The final method of distribution that I will discuss here is distribution based on shares. I am not referring to equity but rather attaching a number of shares to different levels in the organization, typically based on responsibility and impact on organizational performance. For example, administrative and field personnel may receive one share, mid-level management may receive two, and senior leadership may receive three (these are only examples). With this method, the distribution of bonus dollars will be based on the number of shares assigned to the employees given their position in the organization. I am not particularly keen on this method, as it creates something of a "caste" system (or at least the perception of one). It does make sense in some industries, however. Construction-related industries, for example, often adopt this model because there are some organization members (such as project managers) who can have a significant impact on the profitability of the organization and should perhaps have a greater bonus opportunity due to this.

9. Should the Plan Be Quarterly, Annual, or Something Else?

The most effective way to shape behavior is by rewarding it quickly. For this simple reason, I suggest quarterly payout opportunities for most companies as opposed to annual (monthly may be even better, but is typically too difficult to administer). Having said this, I have seen companies get into trouble with quarterly incentive plans. The reason for this is that they do not think the plan through, and therefore they calculate the bonuses the same way every quarter. What would happen if the company has two strong quarters (and therefore large bonus payouts) at the beginning of the year, and then tanks the last two quarters? I suppose you could ask your employees to return their bonus checks (I'm joking, of course). Given the potential of this situation, we simply suggest withholding 50% of the bonus for each of the first three quarters and making an adjustment at year end based on how the company finishes up the year. With this method, and given that the company does not tank, employees would receive roughly one-eighth of their bonus in each of the first three quarters and five-eighths in the last quarter. This allows for a quarterly bonus opportunity while still protecting the cash flow of the company in the event of a downturn.

10. Should There Be a Separate Management Pool?

I have encountered many organizations that feel strongly about providing larger bonus opportunities for leadership, particularly if this is something they have done historically, and/or is common in their industry. In such cases, I will typically acquiesce and design a separate plan for the leadership team. Generally the design is the same as the broad-based plan (with a significantly smaller percentage of PBT paid into the plan), and people in this group will participate in both plans. As an aside, I suggest that if you have a separate leadership pool you communicate this to your employees. If you do not, they will typically find out anyway, and you may have a morale issue to deal with.

I have one final comment on the designs I'm suggesting, which are all based on organizational performance rather than individual performance. A question I hear in nearly every client engagement is "What about the superstars?" In other words, it doesn't seem fair that a slouch would be receiving the same bonus opportunity as a superstar. *This is not an incentive issue; it is a management issue.* In other words, why are you hanging on to the slouch? As Jim Collins says in his book, *Good to Great,* what most companies do is hire quickly and fire slowly. This is always a bad management strategy, but particularly in a company practicing ownership thinking. If someone does not fit, make that determination and take action. If you delay making the difficult decision of terminating someone, it not only hurts the company, but it damages your credibility as a leader. More often than not, when a poor performer is finally terminated, the surrounding employees are thinking "What took them so long?"

Another important point in this regard is that I want to see organizations of excellence, not simply pockets of excellence in an organization. When a bonus plan is tied to organizational performance, and an environment of high visibility is created at the same time, employees become far less tolerant of poor performance. They will typically help an employee with questionable performance either rise to the occasion or find the door. It creates a self-selecting environment. There are other ways to reward superstars: compensation, recognition, and growth opportunities to name a few.

Conclusion

A properly designed incentive plan can have a significant impact on the financial performance of an organization, but keep in mind that the plan itself will not change behavior. The cultural components noted in this chapter (and in my book and NCEO publications such as *The Ownership Edge*) are critical to engaging your employees in driving the performance of the organization so that the financial resources are achieved to ensure the plan is self-funded. In addition, these methods of engaging employees create a far more interesting and challenging work environment, and one that will improve employee satisfaction and retention. Incentives are important, to be sure, but research makes it clear that employees rarely leave a company solely because of money.

CHAPTER 4

Beyond Bribery: Short-Term Incentives That Grow an Ownership Culture

Cathy Ivancic

"Eat your vegetables and you can have dessert," the old saying goes. Does this extrinsic reward—dessert—really motivate anyone to eat vegetables? I know that my children comply with this "incentive" by jamming the remaining zucchini into their mouths and swallowing hard. I did the same to my parents when they offered me this incentive (perhaps you did, too). Obviously, the reward did not create a full understanding of the need for the behavior, nor did it develop a desire to repeat it in the future. No, the "dessert" incentive engendered only temporary compliance, not a real "ownership" of the process.

Leaders in an employee-owned context expect more than compliance from their incentives. I hear my clients declare that they want employees to "think like owners." The leadership is anticipating that installing a short-term incentive will encourage an ownership mentality where employees act like business people who have a stake in company success. But what makes short-term group incentives in employee-owned companies any different from the classic dessert bribe?

Regardless of the noble reasons why leaders implement an incentive, it can be perceived by employees as manipulative or meaningless. The challenge, of course, is getting beyond bribery. In this chapter, I will explore the design elements that are important to make an effective short-term incentive and then look at the implementation of the bonus programs that work.

Do Short-Term Incentives Make Ownership Real?

Employee ownership's greatest strength—a shared interest in long-term performance—is also its greatest weakness. Equity ownership has drawbacks as an incentive. First, the rewards are not timely, and second, the connection to daily work is difficult to see. This is particularly true where the value of the equity is realized at retirement, such as in an employee stock ownership plan (ESOP). In addition, equity compensation that does not require any up-front commitment of dollars from employees may not seem real. With no "skin in the game," it is entirely possible for employees to consider the equity reward "funny money." Short-term incentives are frequently implemented as a strategy to bring the reality of these future rewards into the present—that is, to make ownership "real."

If you reward people for current performance results, so the thinking goes, they will be more aware of how the business is doing and pay attention to performance. Among the strongest advocates of short-term incentives are companies that describe themselves as "open-book" firms. Some employee-owned companies point to their bonus programs as linchpins of their success—a great way to "communicate business goals."[1] For this group of employee-owned companies, their bonus program is making ownership more meaningful and building their ownership culture.

Unfortunately, for each bonus program that builds a sense of purpose there is the same number of employee-owned firms disappointed with the results of their incentive programs. The story often goes something like this: XYZ Company has an annual bonus tied to performance, such as a percentage of annual net income. In addition, employees also have the long-term benefit of employee ownership. Despite these clear incentives, people have not changed their behavior to act in ways that earn the bonus or grow stock value. Leaders at

1. See John Case, *Open-Book Management: The Coming Business Revolution* (New York: HarperCollins, 1995), Jack Stack and Bo Burlingham, *The Great Game of Business* (New York: Currency Doubleday, 1992) and Jim Bado and Cathy Ivancic Open-Book Management: Developing Employees Business Sense (Menlo Park, Ca: Crisp Publications, 1997) for detailed examples of companies that describe the incentive component of their company culture as an important element of their success.

XYZ Company have posted reports and provided information on the incentive with little result from the apathetic work force. Like children who resist eating vegetables, the employee owners seem to not know or care what is good for them.

Research on rewards supports this notion that rewards can backfire and fail to cultivate an understanding of group purpose. The critics of incentives—including leading organizational thinkers such as W. Edwards Deming—say that rewards can encourage short-term thinking, nourish rivalries, and even damage teamwork.[2] These critiques are most strongly targeted at individual merit pay-for-performance plans, but critiques are also leveled against group incentives such as profit-sharing plans and group bonus systems. Rosabeth Moss Kanter notes that variable incentives are often unconnected to what employees contribute and may put a large part of compensation at risk—a problem for lower-paid employees who cannot afford to take that chance.[3] In *Punished by Rewards,* Alfie Kohn characterizes incentives as manipulations that cultivate shortsighted behavior, encourage orchestration of appearances, and distract from the intrinsic value of doing good work. Kohn argues that even group rewards can muster only "temporary compliance" and will eventually be seen as manipulation.[4] Peter Block contends in his 1993 critique of traditional corporate governance that despite the popular belief to the contrary, the research on rewards indicates that "productivity is not for sale."[5]

If you know you're being manipulated, then it is legitimate to manipulate the system so that you can "win." Hence we observe the

---

2. W. Edwards Deming, *Out of the Crisis* (Cambridge: MIT Center for Advanced Engineering Study, 1986), 102. See also Fredrick Herzberg, "One More Time: How Do You Motivate Employees?" *Harvard Business Review,* January/February 1968, 53–62. Herzberg maintains the answer to this question is that "you don't."

3. See Rosabeth Moss Kanter, *When Giants Learn to Dance* (New York: Simon and Schuster, 1989), 234–237.

4. Alfie Kohn, *Punished by Rewards: The Trouble with Gold Stars, Incentive Plans, A's, Praise, and Other Bribes* (New York: Houghton Mifflin Company, 1993).

5. See Peter S. Block, *Stewardship: Choosing Service over Self-Interest* (San Francisco: Berrett Koehler Publishers, 1993), 167.

tendency for a bonus program to degenerate into people "working" the bonus program.

Consider the ESOP-owned distributor who provided individual bonuses for employees who sell off skids of slow-moving inventory. This program was very successful at reducing inventory levels and freeing up cash. After a few years of this incentive, it became apparent that some people would purchase stock during the year that would not move at a normal markup. They would plan to get a bonus for selling the inventory off at a discount at the end of the year with the bonus program. The incentive became an entitlement. It no longer focused people on business goals, the employees were not thinking like owners, and the bonus exacerbated the problem.

What is the difference between situations where the bonus builds an ownership culture and situations where the bonus in ineffective or damaging?

Select a Design That Fits Your Purpose

Companies have a lot of different reasons to have a variable pay component based on performance (bonus). If you already have a bonus or incentive, consider carefully its current purpose (intended or not intended). Is the bonus a way to teach people about job-level expectations? Do you have it to provide above-market levels of compensation when the company can afford it? Is its real purpose to engender loyalty to your leadership team or the company? Or is it part of your strategy to grow a culture of ownership by teaching people about the big picture of the business?

It is the last purpose, growing a culture of ownership, which I am addressing here, but that is not to say that in any given company there may be incentives with other purposes at work. The challenge is that when these purposes are unrecognized they can work against building shared accountability. For example, a division executive who traditionally hands out large annual bonuses based on subjective criteria may be running a fairly effective (albeit not replicable) performance management system. The bonus is working for motivation, but it has a different function from the kind of short-term incentive that will build "ownership thinking." An honest assessment of the purpose of your incentive will help you to make decisions about the necessary tradeoffs in the design process. After 20 years of working with employee-owned companies, I have come to recognize that an incentive is an imperfect tool. When it comes to design there are tradeoffs. Below are just a few of the inherent tradeoffs. Companies must make choices.

Tradeoff 1: Triggering Payouts Close to the Job Versus Reaching Company-Wide Success

Business is a team sport. If your bonus purpose is to get people thinking like business people, the payout needs to reflect reaching big-picture group goals. I've heard leaders say, "It's not fair to base the bonus on something they really can't control; there are so many factors that employees in the department can't change that affect our profitability." If the purpose of the incentive is to build big-picture thinking and the incentive triggers as a result of a department-level goal, then your communication process has the burden of connecting that to company performance. This is an uphill battle.

If your incentive triggers with company-wide goals, then your implementation must make a connection to job-level performance. People tend to understand their own jobs better than the big picture, so leaning toward a company-wide success trigger is often an effective way to focus on the big picture. But there is a real tradeoff here, and it will be essential to track departmental and individual measures as part of the ongoing communication.

Tradeoff 2: Simplicity Versus Telling the Full Business Story

Being a full participant in an ownership culture requires connecting how daily actions impact departmental results, which impact your division, which ultimately leads to company-wide results. You can build that connection right into the bonus. An incentive can be designed that has both departmental measures, such as reducing waste, increasing return business, or maintaining quality, as well as company-wide measures, such as increasing profit or sales. . This kind of combination design allows for a range of local behaviors to be recognized and rewarded with the real payout tied to company-wide performance goals. This kind of bonus also runs up against another tradeoff in incentive design, which is avoiding undue complexity versus measuring things people see each day.

The HR manager at an employee-owned company with 15 years of dealing with this tradeoff described the experience this way: "We've got a lot of engineers in this company who want to dig into the details and create a perfect model. For a lot of years, we had elaborate incentives that had a percentage based on departmental goals, a part on division objectives and then a range of company-wide goals. Each year we worked very hard on those designs hoping to reflect an individual group's contribution to the company. In the end, we learned that these incentives were just too complex for clear explanation. We have settled on a bonus that triggers anytime results exceed our EBITDA targets." Many of the most successful bonus programs lean toward simplicity. Choosing simplicity means that your incentive does not "tell of the full business story." Therefore, the implementation of the bonus must make up for the flaw of the disconnection to employees' daily experiences.

Tradeoff 3: Self-Funding Risk Versus Timely, Frequent Payout

You'll find a lot of bonus programs that pay out after the end of the fiscal year. This, after all, is a fiscally sound approach. Paying a bonus before you know that your year-end performance will merit the bonus could damage the health of the business. Unfortunately, if the purpose of your incentive is to focus people on how their actions impact the success of the business, there is a strong reason for wanting a timely payout that comes quickly after the behaviors that generated the performance. Let's say you had a great first quarter because employees controlled costs and successfully launched a new product line. If they have to wait for nine months to get the incentive, is your bonus really communicating the connection between actions and results? There is an inherent tradeoff between an incentive being airtight in its ability to "pay for itself" and the timeliness of a payout.

Successful designs tend to lean in the direction of timely, frequent payouts, but they also contain design elements that can mitigate the risk of the payout damaging the business. A bonus can be designed to recognize outstanding performance but kick out smaller payouts until you have reached the year-end goals. For example, a construction company pays out based on filling up a bucket of profits. Every time the company fills up a bucket with $75,000 worth of profits, some bonus is paid. Earlier buckets pay out small amounts, and later buckets pay out large rewards. Another approach is to pay a quarterly bonus that holds back some (such as half) of the payout until the end of the year. Everyone is aware that the bonus was earned, but performance must be met to get the final payout. Other chapters in this book outline the 10-20-30-40 payout approach that accomplishes the same outcome. Your normal business cycle should be considered in order to choose the right mechanism for your company. None of these design approaches, however, can completely eliminate the risk you take on with timely, frequent payouts, but they can reduce the downside of this tradeoff.

These are just a few of the tradeoffs that exist in incentive design. Finding the perfect incentive is not possible. All you can do is select solutions to the inherent tradeoffs while keeping in mind your overall purpose. Many, but not all, successful bonus programs that are part of growing a culture of ownership tend to settle these tradeoffs in the following ways:

- company-wide payout triggers
- simple to explain
- potential payout is frequent (monthly or quarterly)

With that said, the truth is that design is a small part of the equation for success. Many companies choose differently in the above tradeoffs and still have tremendous success. Others can follow all the design rules and fail at growing a sense of ownership. Good design cannot overcome poor communication, but good communication can overcome design obstacles.

Implementation and Communication Is 90% of Success

It isn't the bonus design that is producing an environment for continuous improvement and "owner-like" thinking—it is the implementation and ongoing communication surrounding the plan. I often invite my clients to think of the short-term incentive as an "excuse to pay attention to performance." If it isn't accomplishing this, then it isn't really contributing to building a culture of ownership. If you are stimulating a conversation about performance with your bonus, then it is doing its job.

This means you'll have a great incentive if it *creates meaningful two-way conversation about performance*—even if you break every design suggestion outlined above. Here are a few real-world examples of companies that had great success because they kept in mind the reason for the incentive and let it evolve as a tool for communication.

Consider the Midwestern manufacturer whose incentive has grown increasingly complex over the years; the complexity is a result of learning about the business together. The incentive started with a simple quarterly bonus paid when profit targets were met. Over 10 years, it grew to become a quarterly bonus in which 60% is based on company-wide targets and 40% is based on workgroup targets such as customer service, work order completion, or safety targets. In addition, the company has a different customer service bonus for on-time delivery that could be up to $240 a quarter. The real magic is not in the design, because frankly the design is cumbersome and complex. Because employees widely understand the incentive as "the way we learn about our individual impact," the goal setting process is about raising the bar. Anyone who sandbagged or cheated on local measures would violate the understood reason for the incentive. The power of this bonus is in the conversations in each department about setting the workgroup targets and the routine meetings at a department level about reaching goals, and not in the perfection of its design.

The incentive that will "create a meaningful conversation about performance" in your company just might grow out of starting with the "wrong" design. A job-shop client of ours started the design process focusing on sales volume and margin targets for different categories of customers but eventually the management team settled on a company-wide earnings trigger. If the group had started with the final design, it would have missed the opportunity for the leadership team to have a deep discussion about what really drives the business. Many companies start with one design and morph to something different. Rather than seeing this as a problem of being wrong until we got it right, it is probably a sign that the incentive is serving its most essential function: an excuse to deepen our group's shared understanding about performance.

An Incentive People Can Call Their Own

Employee ownership companies have an advantage over conventionally owned companies because the long-term benefit of equity ownership balances short-term thinking created by an incentive plan. Ownership can create a foundation for seeing an incentive as a step toward a shared goal rather than a manipulative practice. The implementation and communication of the short-term incentives are key elements to achieving this.

When the purpose of the incentive is understood and properly communicated, employees know that it is not management's effort to change or manipulate their behavior; instead, it is a scorecard to show people how they are doing. The specific communication processes implemented in successful companies can be very different, but they have following common characteristics:

Employees, not company leaders, "own" the process. When people talk about group incentives in these companies, they describe them as something the group can influence. The incentive is not a reward bestowed on employees by leaders or a carrot to motivate employees. Leaders do not dish out the rewards. For example, leaders won't take credit for them or give them as a gift. Instead, it is a way of keeping track of shared performance. The bonus is clearly earned.

Incentives are part of building knowledge about business objectives. Successful group incentives are not stand-alone programs; they are expressions of business objectives. These incentives find their way into regular communications, formal education sessions, and informal dialogue about work. When successful companies are asked about how they communicate the bonus or incentive, they generally list every corporate communication channel they have: newsletters, employee training, emails, meetings, performance reviews, and work team tracking. Employees know the reason for the bonus is to teach people about how the company makes money, so it permeates all channels for communication.

People get more than material rewards. Social and emotional rewards come from the fact that people are empowered to affect results. Working together to achieve the reward, using one's creativity to solve problems, and being a part of reaching objectives are personally rewarding. The way an incentive is implemented can help or hinder its ability to generate these nonmaterial rewards for people.

Methods to Help Communicate Group Incentives

What can companies do to begin improving the implementation of their bonus? The ideas below, based on the experiences of more than 50 employee-owned companies throughout the United States that use incentives, can provide a starting point for companies working to move beyond bribery with their incentives.

Include both the numbers and the stories behind the numbers. Develop the skills of leaders throughout your company to communicate about performance in both numbers and stories. Group incentives tied to measurable results are not useful if people do not understand how the measure fits with daily work. Stories paint the picture of how work and the performance numbers fit together. The art of telling the business story must be cultivated throughout the company.

Provide an opportunity for people at all levels to tell their own stories. Top-level leaders need to work to relinquish the job of explaining why the incentive went up or down. Employees need to begin to develop the knowledge and information needed to be able to tell their own stories. Leaders should challenge them to do this by turning the communication about performance into a two-way conversation and creating regular opportunities for the conversation to take place. If your company chooses to do formal training on business concepts, make sure the educational approach goes beyond a standard lecture-style format and challenges people to practice talking about their contribution to performance. You learn the most when you have to do the thinking.

Run communication on a frequent and regular schedule. If an employee only hears about the bonus at the annual meeting, it is difficult to see the connection to daily work. Regular communications (quarterly, monthly, weekly, or even daily) help make the incentive a point of focus for daily activities. Moreover, they provide the repetition needed for learning to take place.

Educate people on how their work affects the numbers. Teach people about how they affect performance. Teaching about company financial statements is not enough. Focus educational efforts—both those that happen in a classroom and in regular company communication—on creating a "line of sight" (i.e., a clearly perceptible connection) between daily work and company performance. Developing a common language for talking about these connections is much more important than knowledge of the accounting rules that create financial statements.

Set objectives for your incentive and invite employees to participate in the process. If there are not clear goals for the incentive plan, it is time to think again about whether the bonus helps develop ownership thinking. Asking employees to help define the goals of the incentive, set the criteria, or establish local objectives within certain parameters helps people "own" the results.

Create opportunities for employees to make improvements that affect performance. Without avenues for employee participation, an incentive cannot be a way to focus actions. Consider the following approaches to excessive overtime. One approach is to set specific policies on when overtime is permitted, and no bonus is paid if the rule is violated. Another would be to explain how overtime is connected to the bonus, set big-picture goals for improvement, track results publicly, and challenge employees to make suggestions and implement changes to avoid excessive overtime. In the first example, the incentive is a reward for following a company policy. In the second example, the incentive is evidence that employees can affect performance. A group incentive is empty without genuine empowerment to make improvements.

Make it fun and engaging. Who made the rule that communication about financial results must be boring and dull? Most of the traditional means for communicating about performance—annual reports, shareholder meetings, or reviews of the financial statements—were originally designed for outsiders. Meeting targets is fun; overcoming business challenges is exciting; working together toward common goals is rewarding. Unfortunately, most companies do not make their communication about these things reflect that excitement. When communicating with insiders, it is fine to break the "rules" by making it into a game, using visual aids and props, making noise, singing, or even jumping up on your chair. Consider that communicating about performance is not much different from other ways of keeping score for a group. An announcer at a football game would never say "on page six of the handout you'll see the detailed spreadsheet that shows Central High has improved yards gained in the second quarter." Keep score on a big board where everyone can see it in real time gets employee owners involved in providing the high-energy commentary.

Beyond Bribery: Who Owns the Results in Your Company?

Short-term group incentives do not always develop a sense of purpose or an "ownership" of the work process. The implementation and communication of group incentives can make a tremendous difference in whether employee owners see the incentive as manipulation—like the "vegetable bribe"—or as a tool for self-improvement.

When employee owners believe that leaders are in control of the game, as in a parent-child relationship, incentives will create temporary compliance at best. When employee owners understand their business and its objectives, incentives can inspire a conversation about performance. When extrinsic incentives help people to track and control their own activities' impact on the whole company, the short-term bonus is a tool to help people take "ownership" of the results of their work. Good design can help you get on the right track, but communication and implementation are the keys to getting beyond bribery.

CHAPTER 5

Bonus Plans and the Great Game of Business

Rich Armstrong

Why do companies develop bonus plans? Some companies create them to attract and retain good employees. Others develop bonus plans to motivate or engage their employees and to reward people for great performance. For the most part, companies develop bonus plans to help them drive improved results. Can they work? The evidence and our experience indicate they can, but only if well-designed and well-executed. But it's important to remember, bonus plans *alone* don't drive improved performance. People drive improved performance. A bonus plan can help improve results only if people clearly understand what improvements are needed, how they can make a difference, and what they stand to gain. Bonus plans are a lot like the accelerator on a car. It won't start the engine, but it will certainly make it go faster, potentially much faster.

At SRC Holdings,[1] we spend a lot of time telling people that business is a game. It has players, rules, winners, and losers. Rewards depend on performance. The difference, of course, is that the stakes are much higher. You're playing for your livelihood, and you're playing for money—potentially, lots of money. What's more, it can be as exciting, as challenging, as interesting, and as much fun as any game you can think of—provided you understand what's going on and how you can directly contribute.

Building on this idea, we use what we call the Great Game of Business to put structure and meaning behind our bonus plans. It's what

1. SRC Holdings is the holding company for a number of businesses created by Springfield ReManufacturing Company, the originator of the Great Game of Business.

makes our bonus plans work. The Great Game of Business is an open-book approach to management where every employee:

- is given the measures of business success and taught to understand them *(they know and teach the rules)*;
- is expected and enabled to act on their knowledge to improve performance *(they follow the action and keep score)*; and
- has a direct stake in the company's success *(they're provided a stake in the outcome)*.

From our experience, if any of these three components are missing in your bonus plan, you might as well give out memberships to the "Jelly of the Month Club" and hope for the best.

This chapter describes the basic features of how the Great Game of Business works.

The Great Game Process

You begin by setting up the game around a *critical number*—a performance target that represents what's most important to the organization and critical to success. It's important to involve everybody in defining the critical number. When goals are created with broad participation—that is the minds of the people who are closest to the action and who understand the realities—it creates a level of commitment and alignment that just can't be matched. When the critical number is correctly identified, targeted, and tied to a performance incentive, the rules of The Game have been set. The critical number becomes the focus of the game. Critical numbers can be many things—sales growth, profit, overhead absorption, billable hours, EBITDA, value added—whatever is essential to defining business success. There may be critical weaknesses you want to address by adding another critical number to the mix, such as quality problems, delayed shipments, accounts receivable days, etc. Critical numbers can exist for the entire company or for parts of the company. You might also change the numbers as problems get resolved or new key drivers emerge.

Next, you do everything you can to educate people about the critical number—what it is, why it's important—so everyone can contribute to achieving it. This may seem like a daunting task, but it doesn't have to be. Critical numbers are straightforward; they are much less complicated than income statements or balance sheets. They are simple scores that can be charted and reported regularly. In sports, most baseball fans understand why earned run average or slugging percentages are critical numbers. Critical numbers in business are no harder to explain.

Next, help people win the game. Encourage people to find ways to communicate and promote the concept. Critical number scoreboards, cascading scorecards, huddles (regular small meetings of employees in various work groups), rolling forecasts, and mini-games (explained later) are just a few of the practices we've developed over the years to support the game. An almost "informal" learning process occurs. Everybody learns, everybody plays, and everybody wins.

Finally, when employees win the game, make sure they are rewarded with a significant portion of the gain. Celebrate the win and recognize the players. Then you do it all over again—steadily refining the process and adding new ways to improve it.

Our experience in the early days is a pretty good example of how we learned to use the game to provide our people a stake in the outcome. Below is an excerpt from *A Stake in the Outcome* (Doubleday, 2002) by Jack Stack that describes those early years developing our bonus plan and refining the game. As you will see, our approach to bonus plans evolved from a sincere belief in the power of creating a business of people who think, act, and feel like owners.

> After a year in business, our financed debt still totaled $7.2 million and cast a shadow over everything we did. We decided we'd shoot for reducing our financed debt by $3 million in the coming year. It was a goal that everybody could understand and get behind, since meeting it would greatly increase the job security of us all.
>
> We also set a target of $2.2 million in pretax profit for the year. Hitting that one would ensure that (a) we didn't sacrifice profitability to meet the debt-reduction goal; (b) we'd have enough cash to pay whatever bonuses we earned; and (c) we'd be able to get people focused on learning about the income statement and its relationship to the balance sheet.
>
> The next step was to come up with a set of rewards for winning the game. We figured that, if we actually hit the two goals, we could afford to pay $300,000 in bonuses, which amounted to about 8 percent of our annual payroll. So that became the bonus pool. Each of us would be playing for a

potential bonus of 8 percent of our pay. [This was roughly an additional one month's pay.]

Of course, there was always the possibility that we'd do well but fall short of the highest target on one of the goals. In that case, we decided, the fair thing would be to pay out a portion of the bonus pool. So we divided the pool between the two goals. (In later years, we went a step further and set different levels of payout depending on how well we did on each goal.)

We also realized that it was important to keep everybody involved in the game throughout the year. So we decided to have specific targets—and potential bonuses—for each quarter. To avoid the possibility of a letdown after a lackluster quarter, however, and to keep the focus on the annual goal, we set up the game to make sure the stakes kept rising as the year went along. In the first quarter, 10 percent of the annual bonus pool would be up for grabs; in the second, another 20 percent; in the third, another 30 percent; and in the last quarter, the remaining 40 percent. We call this the 10-20-30-40 bonus plan.

What's more, any part of the bonus we didn't earn in one quarter would be added to the pot in the next quarter. So even if we fell short in the first three quarters, we could still come back and win it all at the end of the year.

That was the game. There were enough twists in the rules that it wouldn't be boring, but it wasn't so complicated that people wouldn't get it. Our theme for the bonus plan was "Skip-The-Praise-Give-Us-The-Raise" (or STP-GUTR, pronounced "Stop-Gooter"). It was a way of telling people that, much as we wanted to pay them more money, the company couldn't afford any raises unless we hit certain targets. Just to make sure everybody got the message, we put together a chart showing how to translate the payout levels into individual bonuses. [Today we translate the payout levels by percentage of pay, dollars per $10,000 of pay, days of pay, and hours of pay.]

Then the entire team worked overtime to make sure people understood the game and the goals and knew what they had to do to win. In the process, we all became teachers, especially those of us with a somewhat better grasp of the numbers.

For example, we put our standard cost accountant in the middle of production. His job was to teach finance to the people in the plant. He began conducting almost daily tutorials with individual supervisors, going through work orders, showing how the numbers flowed back to the income statement, and how the income statement flowed into the balance sheet. The supervisors then went out and did the same thing with the hourly people. Today we continue this process of train the trainer. It's the most effective way we know of to teach the language of business quickly and effectively.

Meanwhile, the other managers ran training sessions of their own and we talked up the game at every chance we got. Our CFO would regularly go on the public address system to give updates on the score. At the end of each quarter, we'd hold a series of informational meetings throughout the company to review the results with all of the employees.

So the bonus program became a powerful mechanism for informal business training. At the same time, it served as the catalyst for developing a whole series of other mechanisms that became crucial elements of how we managed the business.

The *weekly huddle process,* for example, grew out of our need to stay on top of the numbers and keep everyone informed about our progress in the game. Early on, we began holding weekly meetings at which the department managers would report their numbers for the prior week. With that we could put together a rough income statement, which gave us an indication of how we were doing on the profit goal. The managers would then take the information back to their departments and fill in the people who hadn't been at the meeting. The front-line supervisors would do the same with people on the shop floor.

We soon found that it wasn't enough to get the prior week's numbers. We needed to know what was coming up so we could do something about it. So each week we began having the managers forecast what they expected their month end numbers to be. We could then compare the forecast with the plan to see how we thought we were doing in the game—and later compare the forecast with the actual results to see how much control we had of the numbers. That practice evolved into what we called forward-looking financials.

The STP-GUTR Game was also the catalyst for our High-Involvement Planning practice, whereby we get people throughout the company involved in our planning and budgeting process. I realized that, as long as I and the other senior managers could control the bonus line, we could afford to delegate the planning function. If the budgets we got back were out of line, as they sometimes were, we could use the bonus as an incentive for people to do better. That was far preferable to the usual practice of tearing the budgets apart, which pretty much guarantees that people feel little responsibility and ownership for achieving the plan.

We also used the bonus plan to talk about the ESOP. We explained how people could have a direct influence on the price per share by reducing debt, increasing profits, and doing all the things we were trying to accomplish through the STP-GUTR Game.

Best of all, people were beginning to get it. They understood the game. They could watch the whole process of wealth creation unfold before their eyes. We could see how every person and every department was contributing to the success of the company, and how the success of the company was driving the value of the stock. We were working together, having fun together, making money together and growing together.

Of course, the proof of any bonus plan is in the results, and our results began to look very good as people got into playing the Great Game of Business. In the first STP-GUTR program, we wound up hitting 100 percent of the debt reduction goal and 70 percent of the profit goal and paid out $291,000 in bonuses (an average of $1,500 per person). The next year we did it again. We came up with two new goals, debt-to-equity ratio and net profit before tax and paid out another $420,000 in bonuses.

From Jack Stack and Bo Burlingham, A Stake in the Outcome *(Doubleday, 2002). Reprinted with permission from the Great Game of Business.*

As you can see, initially creating the STP-GUTR Game wasn't a simple, straightforward, step-by-step process. Even today we continue to refine the game. What was interesting is that the game evolved out of our efforts to create a better, more effective bonus plan.

Today, SRC Holdings Corporation (formerly Springfield Remanufacturing Corporation), just celebrated its 25th year in business and as a result of our commitment to improving financial results and the lives of the employees who drive the results we've had a remarkable run. In 1983, the year the business was founded, a share of SRC stock was worth 10 cents. Today, in 2008, a share of stock has an appraised value of $234. During that time, we've grown from $16 million to over $320 million in sales; from 119 to more than 1,200 employees; and from one company to 17. There are some other numbers, however, that get more to the core of our success. In 1983, the company had just 13 shareholders. Today we are 100% employee-owned. This transfer of ownership is what we are most proud of, and the employees of SRC continue to work long and hard to keep the company's promise of "sharing the wealth with those who create the wealth."

So if you're looking for a simple, safe, fair plan, and you aren't too interested in the details of bonus design, you can easily adapt the SRC 10-20-30-40 plan. As you gain experience, you can refine the plan to fit your company and make it your own. The rest of this chapter should help you gain a better understand of SRC's plan and the finer points of designing and executing a successful bonus plan.

Design and Implementation Rules

While the concept of bonus plans may seem simple, implementation and execution require some real work. Here is what I consider the most important design and implementation rules that embody our general philosophy on bonus plans.

Rally People Around a Common Goal

Ensure that everybody remains focused on the same goals. We want people to play together as a team, to pull in the same direction. We want the team to be aware of how much we depend on one another to reach our goals. We want to reinforce cooperation and encourage collective efforts to make the business stronger. At SRC, everybody understands we either win together or we don't win at all. Providing a stake in the outcome is a two-sided process. One side is helping employees understand that when the company wins, they win. The flip side, often overlooked, is critical: management must first understand that when employees win, the company wins.

Stick to Two or Three Goals

An effective bonus plan should focus on improvement in two or three key performance targets, what we call the critical numbers. To be effective, it's important to focus your team around those critical few measures that make all the difference rather than the important many. The critical number should represent a performance issue that, at any given time, is going to have the greatest impact on the business and is absolutely critical to success. These numbers are unique to each company and will often change over time: gross margin, billable hours, return on assets, cash flow, return on sales, customer satisfaction, and so on. At SRC, we will almost always select profit as one of our critical numbers—to ensure people stay focused on making money. And profits are often the only reliable way to fund the bonus payouts. In addition, profit is rarely our only performance issue. The other critical numbers will change from year to year depending on what we see as our biggest vulnerability.

Get Everybody Involved

We want our people to be highly involved in the creation of their incentives. That's why we spend so much time in the high-involvement planning process (SRC's strategic and financial planning approach). It's during the high-involvement planning process that we set the rules of the game. We get everybody together to take stock of our situation, target specific improvements we need to make, and then commit to hitting those targets. We try to ask everybody for input as to what measures and targets they think the bonus should be based upon. The annual bonus plan is the result of these efforts.

Set the Base Critical Number Performance at the Lowest Level That Still Ensures the Company's Long-Term Financial Security

Everybody should understand that the company's financial health is paramount. At SRC, for example, in order to set our baseline (or minimum performance), we first look at how much profit we need for the continued growth and sustainability of the business—working capital such as replacing worn-out equipment, investments in inventory or research and development, growth in receivables, debt reduction, and so on. We also don't want people to forget the real payoff: the generation of wealth in the form of equity. So we always look at what effect our bonus plan will have on the value of our stock.

Watch Cash Flow

The company must have the cash available to pay the bonus. However, you don't want to wait too long between declaring the bonus and paying it, or employees will find it difficult to connect the performance with the reward. The best approach to this challenge we have heard about involved the connection of accounts receivable days and the bonus payout schedule. To ensure cash was available for the bonus payout, this company informed their employees that they would pay the bonus in the number of days equal to the company's current accounts receivable days outstanding. This was brilliant because it became a great learning opportunity for the employees. They now knew that if they could help reduce A/R outstanding, the company would have the cash to pay the bonuses and, best of all, they would receive their bonus checks that much quicker. Now that's a win-win.

Give People a Chance to Win Early and Win Often

Bonus plans should above all motivate people. And what gets people motivated? Winning. The more people win, the more they want to win. So it's important to structure your plan to create some early wins and put people on a winning track from the outset. Start with small, frequent bonus payouts and let them grow as performance continues to improve. One of the most common mistakes companies make is to have just one bonus payout per year. Then they compound the mistake by not announcing the payout amount until long after the year ends, providing no consistent link between performance and the reward. At SRC, we structure the plan so that people have a chance to earn a bonus every three months. We establish quarterly targets and pay out a bonus if we hit the targets. But because we set up incremental payout levels ranging from 1% of salary to 20% of salary, it's possible to receive part of the bonus, even if we don't achieve our stretch goals. The biggest payout still occurs at the end of the year, because we pay an increasing percentage of what is earned each quarter—keeping everybody in the game until the final buzzer sounds. We also support plans such as the Bucket Plan, where payouts can be as frequent as 10 times per year. With the Bucket Plan, you simply fill a series of buckets with a pre-determined amount of profit. When you fill the bucket with profit, a percentage of that bucket is earned as a bonus. Then the bucket is set aside and you start on a new bucket. And like the SRC plan, each new bucket pays out a larger percentage, so that buckets at the end of the year are worth more in bonus than buckets in the beginning.

Make Sure People Have the Opportunity to Take Home a Significant Portion of the Gain

Bonuses simply won't mean much if the rewards aren't proportionate with the effort they're being asked to put out. At SRC, we create a bonus pool that represents a minimum of 50% of the additional profits generated over and above our required baseline performance. We want our employees to have the opportunity to earn as much as 10% to 20% of their annual compensation, which represents one to two months' additional pay. This seems to get people's attention. And because we provide incremental payout levels from 1% to 20%, employees have the opportunity to earn a bonus early and often.

Use the Bonus Plan to Teach People About Business

Your bonus plan can be the most effective education tool you have. Too often, employees don't understand the financial impact of their decisions and actions, or, worse, non-decisions and non-actions. So, by educating people on the critical number and how each and every one of us can contribute to achieving it, we begin to use the bonus plan to teach and educate our people about the business. The objective is to help everybody create a line of sight from what they do every day to the overall financial results of the company.

We always hope for the "upside" in business—steady sales growth, increasing profits, and improved value. Yet this is not always the case. In fact, too few employees understand the risks that always come along with the rewards. In many ways, the game helps us encourage employees to check the entitlement attitude at the door and put the "what's in it for me?" (WIIFM) in the right perspective, which is absolutely critical in any successful bonus plan.

One example of just how well employees got it was the year they voted not to pay themselves as bonus. Jack Stack and Bo Burlingham describe it in detail:

The Year We Voted Not to Pay Ourselves a Christmas Bonus

The test of an education comes when you have to make real-life choices based on what you've learned. We faced one of those moments at the beginning of November 1989, when people had to decide between protecting their equity and paying themselves a Christmas bonus.

We had already missed the first-quarter and second-quarter bonuses. Then, at the end of October, it became clear that we were going to miss the third-quarter bonus as well, for the first time ever. The third-quarter bonus is paid at the end of November, just in time for Christmas shopping, so people were understandably upset about losing it. What made the situation even hairier is that we were off by only .01 on the current ratio.

The supervisors got together and requested a meeting with me. There was grumbling on the shop floor. People had been working very hard all year, coping with some new business that had come in unexpectedly. The supervisors had been cheering them on, encouraging them to go for the bonus. What were the supervisors supposed to do? How could they keep people pumped up for the rest of the year?

I heard them out. I said, "I understand what you're saying, and I'm as interested in morale and motivation as you are. We can go ahead and pay the bonus if you want to. There's a real good chance we're going to hit it in the fourth quarter anyway, so we can just advance the payout from February to November and let people have the money in time for Christmas.

"But you and your people should think carefully before you accept this offer. If we don't hit our targets in the fourth quarter for some reason, we're going to be out the money we've already paid. That money has to come from somewhere. In fact, it will come out of profits. If that happens, our stock value won't go up as much as it should this year. And remember, every dollar in after-tax profits is worth about $10 in stock value. So it's your choice. We can pay the bonus now, or we can wait until we've earned it. You decide."

For the next week, there was an intense debate throughout the company. It took the production chief half an hour to make the five-minute walk across the shop floor to his office every day. People kept stopping him to ask what he thought and to get his help in evaluating the numbers. Everybody was trying to calculate the likelihood of hitting the targets in the fourth quarter.

When I got back together with the supervisors a week later, I asked them what they'd decided. They told me they had conducted a straw pool. About 40 percent of the people wanted to get the bonus; they were mainly the younger workers who had not been in the company long enough to acquire much equity. The other 60 percent preferred to wait until the bonus was earned. "So what's your decision?" I asked. They wanted me to decide. I said, "No way. You're the ones who are going to have to live with the consequences." They voted overwhelmingly against the bonus.

As it turned out, we missed the bonus again in the fourth quarter by .01 percent. So I had another morale problem. I went back to the staff and said, "Okay, I know you're good, and I can't walk away from the fact you've put in four solid quarters without getting a bonus. So what we'll do is keep the old bonus program." That was the first time in seven years that we'd kept the goals from one year to the next, but this one had a higher level. People needed a win. We had to let them prove how good they were. And they pulled away in the first quarter of 1990.

From Jack Stack and Bo Burlingham, A Stake in the Outcome *(Doubleday, 2002). Reprinted with permission from the Great Game of Business.*

Don't Pay the Bonus Unless It Is 100% Earned

The lesson from this is to do everything in your power to help people win. But, don't undermine your bonus plan by paying bonuses when people come up short on their targets just to keep morale up. This is a simple point, but it's critical. The bonus plan should be a tool for connecting people with the realities of the marketplace. It should not be seen as a gift. It should be viewed as a reward people earn by fulfilling their commitments and reaching their goals. Keep your people well-informed and educated on their progress, but don't change the rules. Once you start changing the rules and making exceptions, the ugly entitlement attitude will begin to creep into your organization. And it's very hard to go back.

Always Celebrate the Win and Recognize the Players

One of leadership's most valuable tools for accomplishing company goals and improving employees' quality of life is the simple act of recognition—identifying and acknowledging the performance of the team or individuals who have performed above and beyond expectations. For people to pitch in and really give the challenge their full and immediate attention, they must know, without question, that everybody is in it together and they will be rewarded and recognized appropriately for their efforts. It's not all about pay, although pay is important. It's about enjoying where you work and knowing you are appreciated for the contributions you make. That's why the Great Game of Business is very much about rewarding, celebrating, and recognizing players day in and day out. Don't underestimate the power of simply saying thank you. Regardless of how you structure your bonus payouts, all payouts should be accompanied with a handshake and a personal, sincere thank you. This simple gesture will make all the difference when you ask your team step up for the next challenge.

Small Wins Add Up to Big Wins

Everybody knows the annual bonus goal is out there, and they have their sights set on it. But they also know that they can only reach the goal by acting on the everyday activities that drive or "move the needle" on the critical number. A Great Game of Business practice that helps us keep the spirit alive all year long is the "Mini-Game"—a short-term improvement challenge designed to correct a weakness or pursue an opportunity within the company. Mini-games break the critical number down into the right drivers that make all the difference. Drivers are lead measures that represent the activities that directly influence the critical number. Mini-games include the same elements of the big game—the employees know the rules, follow the action and keep score, and are provided a stake in the outcome. It may be a small game and a small reward or recognition, but every small win puts us that much closer to the big win. Examples might include improving on-time delivery, getting a certain percentage increase in new customers, reducing waste, decreasing energy use, etc. Each game has a relatively short time period, such as three months. Rewards are typically either small cash bonuses or some kind of fun activity (raffle tickets, going out to a ball game, gift cards, etc.)

I'd like to finish up with what I believe is the vital success factor for creating effective and engaging bonus plans.

Communicate, Communicate, Communicate

Poor communication is by far the main reason most bonus plans fail. No matter how brilliant you have been, no matter how well you have selected your goals, no matter how careful you have structured the payout, your plan simply won't motivate and engage people if they simply don't *get it,* or if they can't follow what's happening. At SRC, communicating by the numbers (often referred to as open-book management) is the core of our communication approach. The financial statements are often the only report card in the company that shows the combined efforts and contributions of each and every department and individual within the company. So why not use the financial numbers to bring people together? Bonus plan success will have everything to do with how well we communicate and encourage our people to stay in the game They need to stay focused on their critical numbers, make sure they're acting on the right financial drivers, and persistently—let me repeat—persistently communicate progress by keeping score and following the action day in and day out.

If you want to see our approach to communicating and driving the bonus plan, I invite you to attend one of SRC's weekly financial huddles. A huddle is our weekly ritual of calculating the score. In an SRC huddle, employees track progress, commit to results and continually think about how they can improve those results. Because we have a common goal of improving the bottom line and are working from a common financial scoreboard, we better collaborate between departments and focus our energies on the critical issues of the business. Because we frequently and openly discuss wins and losses, we keep learning and getting better. With this regular, company-wide, big picture review of the business and the financial outlook, each employee and team can account for their actions with a clear understanding of where the risk and opportunities truly lie and how they can directly impact the company outcomes and their rewards. As our CEO, Jack Stack, has said, "When we come out of our weekly huddle, we can see the whole playing field before us, we know who is where, how the game is unfolding, and what each of us has to do to make sure we keep moving closer to the goal line."

Summary

All who directly participate in strengthening the company likely do so because they have some form of a stake in the outcome. They come to work to win, because they know their work is leading to a significant reward, recognition, or ownership in the outcome. However, no matter how large the reward, it is often not the only motivating force for many employees. The real motivator is the fact that they are involved and informed—included in discussions about what's going on with the business and what to do about it. They have a trusted, respected seat at the company's decision-making table. And they know through playing the game, that what they say and do really counts.

CHAPTER 6

A Primer on Sharing Equity with Employees

Corey Rosen

Many companies, both publicly traded and privately held, want to provide employees with a stake in the company as an incentive or reward for their work. While giving employees cash bonuses, profit sharing, extra vacation, a company car, or other perquisites can be very valued, sharing equity is unique in its ability to link the employee's interests to the long-term growth of company value. Because equity plans can so easily be designed to require employees to earn their shares through future years of service or meeting certain performance targets, they also can be ideal mechanisms for getting employees to focus on long-term goals—and to stay around long enough to make sure they are met.

Equity can be shared in a variety of ways:

- Some plans, such as employee stock ownership plans (ESOPs) and 401(k) plans invested in company stock, are benefit plans that must follow rules of the Employee Retirement Income and Security Act of 1974 (ERISA) concerning who gets how much, when they get it, and what rights they have.
- Other plans, such as employee stock purchase plans (ESPPs), must be offered to all employees meeting minimum requirements, but the employee must make the choice to invest in stock, often at a discount and with an opportunity to buy the stock at a price set 3 to 24 months earlier. These plans can be and are used as employee rewards and incentives, but they are not (and cannot be) designed to provide specific employees with specifically tailored incentives.

- Individual equity plans, including stock options, restricted stock and restricted stock units, phantom stock, and stock appreciation rights, can be given to any employee under any set of criteria. In return for this flexibility, these plans do not carry significant tax benefits, with the exception of incentive stock options (ISOs). ISOs can be taxed as capital gains to the employee, but the company then gives up any tax deduction.

This chapter is not a substitute for detailed investigation of the particular plans chosen. All of these plans involve often complex tax, accounting, planning, administration, financing, and feasibility issues. Instead, this chapter provides a very basic overview to help decision-makers understand the array of choices available.

The first part of the chapter looks at individual equity plans; these plans can be used for selective or broad-based plans. The second part looks at plans that are designed to benefit most or all employees. The chapter mainly focuses on plan design and tax issues. Securities law considerations are briefly discussed near the end, but because this is such a complex subject, they are not reviewed in any detail. Accounting issues are extremely complex and varied for different plans and are discussed very briefly here. For more information on accounting concerns, see the NCEO's *Accounting for Equity Compensation* (for individual equity plans and employee stock purchase plans) or *Leveraged ESOPs and Employee Buyouts* (for ESOPs).

Basic Forms of Individual Equity Plans

There are four basic kinds of individual equity compensation plans: stock options, restricted stock and restricted stock units, stock appreciation rights, and phantom stock. Many of these plans have variations as well. Each plan provides employees with some special consideration in price or terms. We do not cover here simply offering employees the right to buy stock as any other investor would receive or making unrestricted grants of shares.

Stock options give employees the right to buy a number of shares at a price fixed at grant for a defined number of years into the future. *Restricted stock* and its close relative *restricted stock units* give employees the right to acquire or receive shares, by gift or purchase, once certain restrictions, such as working a certain number of years or meeting a performance target, are met. *Phantom stock* pays a future cash bonus equal to the value of a certain number of shares. *Stock appreciation rights* provide the right to the increase in the value of a designated number of shares, usually paid in cash but occasionally settled in shares (this is called a "stock–settled" SAR).

Stock Options

A few key concepts help define how stock options work:

- *Exercise:* The purchase of stock with an option.
- *Exercise price*: The price at which the stock can be purchased. This is also called the *strike price*. In most plans, the exercise price is the current fair market value of the stock at the time the exercise is made.
- *Grant price*: How much the option holder must pay to exercise the option.
- *Spread*: The difference between the grant price and exercise price at the time of exercise.
- *Option term*: The amount of time the employee can hold the option prior to its expiring.
- *Vesting*: The requirement, usually in years of service, that must be met for an option holder to be able to exercise an option.

A company grants an employee options to buy a stated number of shares at a defined grant price. The options vest over a period of time or once certain individual, group, or corporate goals are met. Once vested, the employee can exercise the option at the grant price at any time over the option term up to the expiration date. For instance, an employee might be granted the right to buy 1,000 shares at $10 per share. The options vest 25% per year over four years and have a term of 10 years. If the stock goes up, the employee will pay $10 per share to buy the stock. The difference between the $10 grant price and the exercise price is the spread. If the stock goes to $25 after seven years, and the employee exercises all options, the spread would be $15 per share.

Kinds of Options

Option plans are either incentive stock options (ISOs) or nonqualified options (NSOs). When an employee exercises a nonqualified stock option, the spread on exercise is taxable to the employee as ordinary income, even if the shares are not yet sold. A corresponding amount is deductible by the company. There is no legally required holding period for the shares after exercise, although the company may impose one. Any subsequent gain or loss on the shares after exercise is taxed as capital gains or losses.

An incentive stock option (ISO) enables an employee to (1) defer taxation on the option from the date of exercise until the date of sale of the underlying shares and (2) to pay tax at capital gains rates, rather than ordinary income tax rates, on the spread at exercise. Certain conditions must be met to qualify for ISO treatment:

- The employee must hold the stock for at least one year after the exercise date or two years after the grant date, whichever is later.
- Only $100,000 of stock options can become exercisable in any year. This is measured by the grant price of the options, not the exercise price. It means that only $100,000 in grant price value can vest (first become exercisable) in any one year. If there is overlapping vesting, such as would occur if options are granted annually and vest gradually, companies must track outstanding options to see if the amount that becomes vested under different grants would exceed $100,000 in grant value in any one year.
- The exercise price must be equal to at least 100% of the market price of the company's stock on the date of the grant.
- Only employees can qualify for an ISO.
- The option must be granted pursuant to a written plan that has been approved by shareholders, that specifies how many shares can be issued under the plan, and that identifies the class of employees

eligible to receive the options. Options must be granted within 10 years of the date of the adoption of the plan.

- The option must be exercised within 10 years of the date of the grant.
- The employee cannot own, at the time of the grant, more than 10% of the voting power of all outstanding stock of the company, unless the exercise price is at least 110% of the market value of the stock on the date of the grant, and the option is not exercisable more than five years from the date of the grant.

If all the rules for ISOs are met at the time of exercise, then the transaction is called a "qualifying disposition" and the employee pays capital gains tax on the total increase in value at sale over the grant price. However, the spread on the option at exercise is a "preference item" for purposes of the alternative minimum tax (AMT). So even though the shares may not have been sold, the exercise requires the employee to add back the gain on exercise, along with other AMT preference items, to see if an alternative minimum tax payment is due.

The company does not take a tax deduction when there is a qualifying disposition. If, however, there is a disqualifying disposition, most often because the employee exercises and sells before meeting the required holding periods, the spread on exercise is taxable to the employee at ordinary income tax rates, and any capital appreciation on the ISO shares in excess of the market price on exercise of an ISO is taxed at capital gains rates. In this instance, the company may then deduct the spread on exercise.

Exercising an Option

There are four ways to exercise a stock option: cash, the exchange of existing shares (often called a stock swap), same-day sales, and their close relative, sell-to-cover sales (these latter two are often called cashless exercises, although that term actually includes other kinds of exercise methods described here as well). Any one company, however, may provide for just one or two of these alternatives. Private companies do not offer same-day or sell-to-cover sales, and, not infrequently, restrict the exercise or sale of the shares acquired through exercise until the company is sold or goes public.

The most common form of exercise for an option in a closely held company is simply for the employee to pay cash for the shares. The employee might then have additional taxes due, depending on the kind of option. If the options are nonqualified, the employer might then have to withhold taxes on the spread from the employee's future paychecks, unless the employer can arrange to use some of the option shares to pay for this obligation, as would normally be the case in the kind of cashless transactions described below.

In a same-day sale, the employee works with a broker, usually one provided by the company. The company provides the broker with enough shares to cover the option exercise, the broker turns around and sells them, and the proceeds, minus the exercise price and any taxes due, go to the employee. Although called a "same-day" sale, the process can take up to three days. In a sell-to-cover exercise, the same approach is used, but the broker sells only enough shares to cover the exercise price and any taxes due, giving the employee the remaining value in shares.

In a stock swap, the employee simply exchanges existing shares for the option shares. For instance, if the employee has the right to buy 1,000 shares at $10 per share, and the shares are now worth $25, the employee would exchange 400 shares the employee currently owns for the 1,000 shares. That's because the 400 shares the employee owns are worth $10,000. The employee would then get 600 shares from the option. If there are taxes due, then the employee might choose to turn in enough shares to cover the taxes as well, although this would not be a common strategy. Stock swaps are more commonly used with incentive stock options where taxes do not have to be paid until the newly acquired shares are sold.

Accounting

Under accounting rules for equity compensation plans that became effective in 2006, companies must calculate the present value of all option awards as of the date of grant and show this as a charge to compensation. The value should be adjusted based on vesting experience (so unvested shares do not count as a charge to compensation).

Restricted Stock

Restricted stock provides the employee with the right to purchase shares at fair market value or a discount, or simply grants shares to employees outright. However, the shares employees acquire are not really theirs yet—they cannot take possession of the shares until specified restrictions lapse. Most commonly, the restriction is that the employee work for the company for a certain number of years, often three to five. The time-based restrictions may pass all at once or gradually. Any restrictions could be imposed, however. The company could, for instance, restrict the shares until certain corporate, departmental, or individual performance goals are achieved. With restricted stock units (RSUs), employees do not actually buy or receive shares *until* the restrictions lapse. In effect, RSUs are like phantom stock settled in shares instead of cash.

While the shares are subject to restrictions, companies can choose whether to pay dividends, provide voting rights, or give the employee other benefits of being a shareholder. When employees are awarded the restricted stock, they have the right to make what is called an "83(b)" election (named after Section 83(b) of the Internal Revenue Code), much as they can make this election for a stock option. If they make the election, they are taxed at ordinary income tax rates on the "bargain element" of the award at the time of grant. If the shares are simply granted to the employee, then the bargain element is their full value. If some consideration is paid, then the tax is based on the difference between what is paid and the fair market value at the time of the grant. If full price is paid, there is no tax. Any future increase in the value of the shares until they are sold is then taxed as capital gains, not ordinary income. If employees do not make the election, then there is no tax until the restrictions lapse, at which time ordinary income tax is due on the difference between the grant and exercise price. Subsequent changes in value are capital gains (or losses). RSUs do not allow employees to make the 83(b) election.

The employer gets a tax deduction only for amounts employees pay income tax on, regardless of whether an 83(b) election is made or not. An 83(b) election carries some risk. If the employee makes the election and pays tax but the restrictions never lapse, the employee does not get the taxes paid refunded, nor does the employee get the shares.

Restricted stock accounting parallels option accounting in most respects. If the only restriction is vesting, companies account for restricted stock by first determining the total compensation cost at the time the award is made. So if the employee is simply given 1,000 restricted shares worth $10 per share, then a $10,000 cost is incurred. If the employee buys the shares at fair value, no charge is recorded; if there is a discount, that counts as a cost. The cost is then amortized over the period of vesting until the restrictions lapse. Because the accounting is based on the initial cost, companies with a low share price will find that a vesting requirement for the award means their accounting charge will be very low even if the stock price goes up.

If the award is more contingent, such as performance vesting, the value must be adjusted each year for the current stock price, then amortized over the estimated life of the award (the time estimated to meet the performance goal). Each year, the expected cost is amortized over the estimated remaining expected life. So if the stock is awarded at $10 and goes to $15 in the first year of an expected five-year term, then $15 x 1,000 x .20 is recorded ($3,000). If the price goes to $18 the next year, the calculation is $18 x 1,000 x .40 ($3,600). The prior $2,000 is subtracted from this amount, yielding a charge of $1,800 for that year.

Phantom Stock and Stock Appreciation Rights

Stock appreciation rights (SARs) and phantom stock are very similar plan types. Both essentially are cash bonus plans, although some plans pay out the benefits in the form of shares. SARs typically provide the employee with a cash payment based on the increase in the value of a stated number of shares over a specific period of time. Phantom stock provides a cash or stock bonus based on the value of a stated number of shares, to be paid out at the end of a specified period of time. SARs may not have a specific settlement date; like options, the employees may have flexibility in when to choose to exercise the SAR. Phantom stock may pay dividends; SARs would not. When the payout is made, it is taxed as ordinary income to the employee and is deductible to the employer. Some phantom plans condition the receipt of the award on meeting certain objectives, such as sales, profits, or other targets. These plans often call their phantom stock performance units

Because SARs and phantom plans are essentially cash bonuses or are delivered in the form of stock that holders will want to cash in, companies need to figure out how to pay for them. Does the company just make a promise to pay or does it really put aside the funds? If the award is paid in stock, is there a market for the stock? If it is only a promise, will employees believe the benefit is as phantom as the stock? If it is in real funds set aside for this purpose, the company will be putting after-tax dollars aside and not in the business. Many small, growth-oriented companies cannot afford to do this. The fund can also be subject to excess accumulated earnings tax. On the other hand, if employees are given shares, the shares can be paid for by capital markets if the company goes public or by acquirers if the company is sold.

If phantom stock or SARs are irrevocably promised to employees, it is possible the benefit will become taxable before employees actually receive the funds. A "rabbi trust," a segregated account to fund deferred payments to employees, may help solve the accumulated earnings problem, but if the company is unable to pay creditors with existing funds, the money in these trusts goes to them. Telling employees their right to the benefit is not irrevocable, or is dependent on some condition (working another five years, for instance), may prevent the money from being currently taxable, but it may also weaken employee belief that the benefit is real.

Finally, if phantom stock or SARs are intended to benefit most or all employees and defer some or all payment until termination or later, they may be considered a de facto "ERISA plan." ERISA (the Employee Retirement Income and Security Act of 1974) is the federal law that governs retirement plans. It does not allow non-ERISA plans to operate like ERISA plans, so the plan could be ruled subject to all the constraints of ERISA. Similarly, if there is an explicit or implied reduction in compensation to get the phantom stock, there could be securities issues involved, most likely anti-fraud disclosure requirements. Plans designed just for a limited number of employees, or as a bonus for a broader group of employees that pays out annually based on a measure of equity, would most likely avoid these problems. Moreover, the regulatory issues are "gray areas"; it could be that a company could use a broad-based plan that pays over longer periods or at departure and not ever be challenged.

Phantom stock and SAR accounting is straightforward. These plans would be treated in the same way as deferred cash compensation. As the amount of the liability changes each year, an entry is made for the amount accrued. A decline in value would create a negative entry. These entries are not contingent on vesting. In closely held companies, share value is often stated as book value. As the discussion on valuation in a subsequent chapter shows, however, this can dramatically underrate the true value of a company, especially one based primarily on intellectual capital. Having an outside appraisal performed, therefore, can make the plans much more accurate rewards for employee contributions.

Deferred Compensation Issues for Individual Equity Plans

Employees traditionally were able to defer the receipt of a vested (and thus taxable) equity award under deferred compensation plans by making an election. Rules for how to do this were ambiguous. Tax law changes in 2004 clarified this issue. Under the deferred compensation rules of Section 409A, employees can elect to defer only if several conditions are met:

1. The employee dies, becomes disabled, there is a change in control, there is an unforeseen emergency (as rigorously defined in the law), or there is a fixed date or schedule specified by the plan.
2. Elections for deferral must be made not later than the close of the preceding taxable year in which the award would vest or, if made in the first year of the award, within 30 days after the employee first becomes eligible for an award. If the employee is a key employee (as defined by statute) of a public company, receipt of the benefit must be not earlier than six months after separation.
3. If the award is performance-based, the election must come not later than six months before the end of the performance period.
4. There can be no acceleration of benefits once a deferral election has been made.

5. Any subsequent elections for an award must be at least 12 months after the prior election and must defer receipt for at least five years in the future.

Section 409A's deferred compensation rules do not apply to qualified benefit plans, such as ESOPs or 401(k) plans, as well as sick leave, death benefits, and similar arrangements. Incentive stock options are exempt from Section 409A coverage, as are nonqualified options, provided they are not issued at less than fair market value. Restricted stock is not subject to Section 409A's deferred compensation rules, but restricted stock units are.

Employee Stock Purchase Plans

Millions of employees become owners in their companies through employee stock purchase plans (ESPPs). Many of these plans are organized under Section 423 of the Internal Revenue Code and thus are often called "Section 423 plans." Other ESPPs are "nonqualified" plans, meaning they do not have to meet the special rules of Section 423 and do not get any of the special tax treatment.

Under Section 423, companies generally must allow all employees to participate (except 5%-or-more owners, who must be excluded) but can exclude those with less than two years' tenure, part-time employees, and highly compensated employees. All employees must have the same rights and privileges under the plan, although companies can allow purchase limits to vary with relative compensation (most do not do this, however). Plans can limit how much employees can buy, and the law limits it to $25,000 per year.

Section 423 plans operate by allowing employees to have deductions taken out of their pay on an after-tax basis. These deductions accumulate over an "offering period." At a specified time or times employees can choose to use these accumulated deductions to purchase shares or they can get the money back. Plans can offer discounts of up to 15% on the price of the stock. Most plans allow this discount to be taken based on *either* the price at the beginning or the end of the offering period (the so-called "look-back feature"). The offering period can last up to five years if the price employees pay for their stock is based on the share price at the end of the period or 27 months if it can be determined at an earlier point.

Plan design can vary in a number of ways. For instance, a company might allow employees a 15% discount on the price at the end of the offering period but no discount if they buy shares based on the price at the beginning of the period. Some companies offer employees interim opportunities to buy shares during the offering period. Others provide smaller discounts. Offering periods also vary in length. NCEO studies, however, show that the large majority of plans have a look-back feature and provide 15% discounts off the share price at the beginning or end of the offering period. Most of the plans have a 12-month offering period, with 6 months the next most common.

The tax treatment of a Section 423 plan is similar to that of an incentive stock option plan. If employees hold the shares for two years after grant and one year after exercise, they pay ordinary income tax on the lesser of (1) the discount element as of the beginning of the offering period and (2) the amount by which the sale price exceeds the purchase price. Any additional gain is taxed as a long-term capital gain. The company gets no tax deduction, even on the 15% discount. There is no withholding requirement on the gain on the employee purchase of shares.

If these rules are not met, employees pay ordinary income tax on the entire difference between the purchase price and the exercise price, plus long-term or short-term capital gains taxes on any increase in value over the purchase price. The company gets a tax deduction for the spread between the purchase price and the exercise price.

Nonqualified ESPPs usually work much the same way, but there are no rules for how they must be structured and no special tax benefits. The employee would pay tax on the discount as ordinary income *at the time the stock is purchased* and would pay capital gains on any subsequent gain.

ESPPs are found almost exclusively in public companies because the offering of stock to employees requires compliance with costly and complex securities laws. Closely held companies can, and sometimes do, have these plans, however. Offerings of stock only to employees can qualify for an exemption from securities registration requirements at the federal level, although they will have to comply with anti-fraud disclosure rules and, possibly, state securities laws as well. If they do offer stock in a stock purchase plan, it is highly advisable they obtain at least an annual appraisal.

ESPPs are very popular in public companies and some pre-IPO companies (where the plan starts before the IPO, and purchases are not made until after it) as they offer a benefit to employees and additional capital to companies. Any dilution resulting from the issuance of new shares to satisfy the purchase requests, or from the company repurchasing outstanding shares and reselling them at a discount, is usually so small that shareholders do not object. Rates of participation vary widely, with the median levels around 30% to 40% of eligible employees. Because most employees do not commit large amounts to these plans, and many do not participate at all, ESPPs should generally be seen as an adjunct to other employee ownership plans, not a means in themselves to create an ownership culture.

ESPPs must be accounted for in the same way as options. Any discount offered counts as a compensation charge, and the present value of the option element must be calculated as an additional charge to income.

Employee Stock Ownership Plans (ESOPs)

An ESOP is a kind of employee benefit plan under ERISA. ESOPs were given a specific statutory framework in 1974. Like other tax-qualified deferred compensation plans, they must not discriminate in their operations in favor of highly compensated employees, officers, or owners. In an ESOP, a company sets up an employee benefit trust, which it funds by contributing cash to buy company stock, contributing shares directly, or having the trust borrow money to buy stock, with the company making contributions to the plan to enable it to repay the loan. Generally, at least all full-time employees with a year or more of service are in the plan. Employees almost never contribute to the plan; instead, contributions are funded by the company as a benefit and allocated to employee accounts on a nondiscriminatory basis, much as in a profit sharing plan. To assure that these rules are met, ESOPs must appoint a trustee to act as the plan fiduciary. This can be anyone, although larger companies tend to appoint an outside trust institution, while smaller companies typically appoint a manager or create an ESOP trust committee. ESOPs are designed to invest primarily in the stock of the employer and can buy shares for exiting owners, treasury shares, or newly issued shares.

An ESOP can be used for many purposes, including the following:

- The most common application for an ESOP is *to buy the shares of a departing owner of a closely held company.* Owners can defer tax on the gain they have made from the sale to an ESOP if the ESOP holds more than 30% of the company's stock (and certain other requirements are met). Moreover, the purchase can be made in pretax corporate dollars.
- ESOPs are also used *to divest or acquire subsidiaries, buy back shares from the market (including public companies seeking a takeover defense), or restructure existing benefit plans* by replacing current benefit contributions with a leveraged ESOP.
- Companies can use an ESOP *to buy newly issued shares in the company, with the borrowed funds being used to buy new productive capital.* The company can, in effect, finance growth or acquisitions in pretax dollars while these same dollars create an employee benefit plan.
- Finally, an ESOP can simply be *an employee benefit plan* for companies that want to share ownership broadly. In public companies especially, an ESOP contribution is often used as part or all of a match to employee deferrals to a 401(k) plan.

Funding

The most sophisticated use of an ESOP is to borrow money (a "leveraged" ESOP). The company borrows money from a lender and reloans it to the ESOP; the ESOP uses the money to buy shares. The company makes tax-deductible contributions to the trust to enable it to repay the loan. The company can also used dividends on the shares to repay the loan; these dividends become deductible to the company. In effect, the parallel loan structure allows the company to borrow money to acquire stock and, by funneling the loan through the ESOP, deduct both principal and interest. Proceeds from the loan can be used by the company for any legitimate business purpose. Sellers to an ESOP can also be lenders. The stock is put into a "suspense account," where it is released to employee accounts as the loan is repaid.

The ESOP can also be funded directly by discretionary corporate contributions of cash to buy existing shares or simply by the contribution of shares. These contributions are tax-deductible, generally up to 25% of the pay of the total payroll of plan participants.

How Shares Get to Employees

The rules for ESOPs are similar to the rules for other tax-qualified plans in terms of participation, allocation, vesting, and distribution, but several special considerations apply. All employees over age 21 who work for more than 1,000 hours in a plan year must be included in the plan, unless they are covered by a collective bargaining unit (and the ESOP issues are negotiated in good faith), are in a separate line of business with at least 50 employees not covered by the ESOP, or fall into one of several limited anti-discrimination exemptions.

Shares are allocated to individual employee accounts based on relative compensation (generally, all W-2 compensation is counted), on a more level formula (such as per capita or seniority), or some combination. The allocated shares are subject to vesting. Employees must be 100% vested after three years of service ("cliff" vesting), or the company can use a graduated vesting schedule not slower than 20% after two years and 20% per year more until 100% is reached after six years.

When employees reach age 55 and have 10 years of participation in the plan, the company must offer them a six-year period in which they can diversify company stock in their account balances (in some plans, the plan may be written so they can diversify everything in the account, but the law only requires that the plan allow company stock to be diversified). The company can either give them the option of diversifying 25% of their relevant account balances among at least three other investment alternatives, or simply pay the amount out to the employees. After five years of diversification, employees can have 50% diversified or distributed to them in the sixth year. In public companies where an ESOP and 401(k) plan are combined, employees must be able to diversify their accounts much sooner.

When employees retire, die, or are disabled, the company must distribute their vested shares to them not later than the last day of the plan year following the year of their departure. For employees leaving before reaching retirement age, distribution must begin not later than the last day of the sixth plan year following their year of separation from service. Payments can be in substantially equal installments out of the trust over five years, or in a lump sum. In the installment method, a company normally pays out a portion of the stock from the trust each year.

Closely held companies and some thinly traded public companies must repurchase the shares from departing employees at their fair market value, as determined by an independent appraiser. This so-called "put option" can be exercised by the employee in one of two 60-day periods, one starting when the employee receives the distribution and the second period one year after that. The employee can choose which one to use. This obligation should be considered at the outset of the ESOP and factored into the company's ability to repay the loan.

Rules and Limitations

Shares in the plan are held in individual employee accounts. As contributions are made, they are allocated to each participant in the plan. If there is an ESOP loan, as the loan is repaid, these shares are released to the accounts of plan participants, based either on the principal paid or the percentage of total principal plus interest due that is paid that year. The amount *contributed* to repay the principal on the loan is what counts for determining if the company is within the limits for contributions allowed each year and for the purpose of calculating the tax deduction. The value of the shares released, however, is the amount used on the income statement, where it counts as a compensation cost.

Limitations on Contributions

Congress was generous in providing tax benefits for leveraged ESOPs, but there are limits. Generally, companies can deduct up to 25% of the total eligible payroll of plan participants to cover the principal portion of the loan and can deduct all of the interest they pay. Eligible pay is essentially all the pay (including employee deferrals into benefit plans) of people actually in the plan of $245,000 per participant or less (in 2009 dollars). However, company contributions to other defined contribution plans, such as stock bonus, 401(k), or profit sharing plans, must be counted in this 25% of pay calculation. On the other hand, "reasonable" dividends paid on shares acquired by the ESOP can be used to repay the loan, and these are not included in the 25% of pay calculations. If employees leave the company before they have a fully vested right to their shares, their forfeitures, which are allocated to everyone else, are not counted in the percentage limitations. If the ESOP does not borrow money, the annual contribution limit is now also 25% of covered pay. Again, contributions to other plans reduce this amount.

There are a number of limitations to these provisions, however. First, no one ESOP participant can get a contribution of more than 100% of pay in any year from the principal payments on the loan or the direct ESOP contributions made that year that are attributable to that employee, or more than $49,000 (in 2009 dollars), whichever is less. In figuring payroll, pay over $245,000 per year (in 2009 dollars) does not count toward total contribution limits. Second, if there are other qualified benefit plans, these must be taken into account when assessing this limit. This means that employee deferrals into 401(k) plans, as well as other employer contributions to 401(k) plans, stock bonuses, or profit sharing plans, are added to the ESOP contribution and cannot exceed 100% of pay or $49,000 (in 2009 dollars) in any year.

Third, allocations attributable to repayment of the interest on an ESOP loan are excludable from the individual limits only if not more than one-third of the ESOP's benefits are allocated to highly compensated employees, as defined by the Internal Revenue Code (section 414 (q)). If the one-third rule is not met, forfeitures are also counted in determining how much an employee is getting each year.

In private companies, employees must be able to direct the trustee as to the voting of shares *allocated* to their accounts on several key issues, including closing, sale, liquidation, recapitalization, and other issues having to do with the basic structure of the company. They do not, however, have to be able to vote for the board of directors or other typical corporate governance issues, although companies can voluntarily provide these rights. Instead, the plan trustee votes the shares, usually at the direction of management. In listed corporations, employees must be able to vote on all issues.

Voting

What these rules mean is that for almost all ESOP companies, governance is not really an issue unless they want it to be. If companies want employees to have only the most limited role in corporate governance, they can; if they want to go beyond this, they can as well. In practice, companies that do provide employees with a substantial governance role find that it does not result in dramatic changes in the way the company is run.

Finally In closely held companies and some thinly traded listed companies, all ESOP transactions must be based on a current appraisal by an independent, outside valuation expert.

Tax Benefits to the Selling Shareholder

One of the major benefits of an ESOP for closely held firms is section 1042 of the Internal Revenue Code. Under it, a seller to an ESOP may be able to qualify for a deferral of taxation of the gain made from the sale. Several requirements apply, the most significant of which are:

1. The seller must have held the stock for three years before the sale.
2. The stock must not have been acquired through options or other employee benefit plans.
3. After the sale, the ESOP must own 30% or more of the value of the shares in the company and must continue to hold this amount for three years unless the company is sold. Shares repurchased by the company from departing employees do not count.
4. Shares qualifying for the deferral cannot be allocated to accounts of the selling shareholder(s); certain close relatives of the selling shareholder(s), such as children, brothers or sisters, spouses, or parents; or more-than-25% shareholders.
5. The company must be a C corporation.

If these rules are met, the seller (or sellers) can take the proceeds from the sale and reinvest them in "qualified replacement securities" within 12 months after the sale or 3 months before and defer any capital gains tax until these new investments are sold. Qualifying replacement securities are defined essentially as stocks, bonds, warrants, or debentures of domestic corporations receiving not more than 25% of their income from passive investment. Mutual funds and real estate trusts do not qualify. If the replacement securities are held until death, they are subject to a step-up in basis, so capital gains taxes would never be paid.

Increasingly, lenders are asking for replacement securities as part or all of the collateral for an ESOP loan. This strategy may be beneficial to sellers selling only part of their holdings because it frees the corporation to use its assets for other borrowing and could enhance the future value of the company.

Corporate Tax Benefits

As noted, companies can use ESOPs to borrow money and repay the loan entirely in pre-tax dollars. In addition, companies can take a tax deduction for reasonable dividends used to repay a loan, that are passed through directly to employees, or that employees voluntarily reinvest in company stock. Contributions not used to pay an ESOP loan are tax-deductible as well, even if made in the form of treasury or new shares.

ESOPs in S Corporations

While ESOPs in S corporations operate under most of the same rules as in a C corporation, there are important differences.

Interest payments on ESOP loans count toward the contribution limits (they normally do not in C companies). Dividends (called "distributions" in S corporations) paid on ESOP shares are also not deductible. Most important, sellers to an ESOP in an S corporation do not qualify for the tax-deferred rollover treatment.

On the other hand, the ESOP is unique among S corporation owners in that it does not have to pay federal income tax on any profits attributable to it (state rules will vary). This can make an ESOP very attractive in some cases. It also makes converting to an S corporation very appealing when a C corporation ESOP owns a high percentage of the company's stock.

For owners who want to use an ESOP to provide a market for their shares, generally it will make sense to convert to C status before setting up an ESOP. Where selling shares is not a priority, or where the seller either does not have substantial capital gains taxes due on the sale or has other reasons to prefer staying an S corporation, an S ESOP can provide significant tax benefits. However, owners must keep in mind that any distributions paid to owners must be paid pro-rata to the ESOP. The ESOP can use these distributions to purchase additional shares, to build up cash for future repurchases of employee shares, or just to add to employee accounts.

While the S corporation rules make an ESOP very attractive, legislation passed in 2001 makes it clear that these rules are not meant to be abused by companies seeking to create the ESOP primarily to benefit a few people. For instance, some accountants were promoting plans in which a company would set up an S corporation management company owned by just a few people that would manage a large C corporation. The profits would flow through the S corporation, which would then not be taxed.

The rules Congress enacted are complicated, but they boil down to two essential points. First, people who own 10% or more of the "deemed-owned shares" of the company, or 20% counting their family members, are considered "disqualified" persons. "Deemed-owned" shares include synthetic equity (phantom stock, SARs, and many forms of deferred cash compensation or other rights to corporate assets), allocated shares in the ESOP, and a proportionate share of unallocated shares. Second, if these disqualified people together own 50% or more of the company's stock, counting deemed-owned shares, shares counted under attribution of ownership rules, and shares held directly, then no portion of the assets of the ESOP company can accrue to them under the ESOP, or be allocated to any other qualified plan of the employer, for the benefit of the disqualified person without extraordinary tax penalties. Congress also directed the IRS to apply this onerous tax treatment to any plan it deems to be substantially for the purpose of evading taxes rather than providing employee benefits.

Financial Issues for Employees

When an employee receives a distribution from the plan, it is taxable unless rolled over into an IRA or other qualified plan. Otherwise, the amounts contributed by the employer are taxable as ordinary income, while any appreciation on the shares is taxable as capital gains. In addition, if the employee receives the distribution before normal retirement age and does not roll over the funds, a 10% excise tax is added.

While the stock is in the plan, however, it is not taxable to employees. It is rare, moreover, for employees to give up wages to participate in an ESOP or to purchase stock directly through a plan (this raises difficult securities law issues for closely held firms). Most ESOPs either are in addition to existing benefit plans or replace other defined contribution plans, usually at a higher level of pay.

Accounting

In nonleveraged plans, the contribution to the ESOP shows up directly as a compensation cost. In leveraged plans, the principal payments and dividends paid on unallocated shares to repay a loan show up as a compensation charge as well; dividends on allocated shares show up as a charge to retained earnings. The debt of the ESOP shows up as corporate debt, with an offsetting contra equity account that is reduced as the loan is repaid.

401(k) Plans

Company stock is a common component of 401(k) plans in public companies and, occasionally, closely held companies. There are several factors that favor the use of a 401(k) plan as a vehicle for employee ownership in public firms. From the company's perspective, its own stock may be one of the most cost-effective means of matching employee contributions. If there are existing treasury shares or the company prints new shares, contributing them to the 401(k) plan may impose no immediate cash cost on the company; in fact, it would provide a tax deduction. Other shareholders would suffer a dilution, of course. If the company has to buy shares to fund the match, at least the dollars are being used to invest in itself rather than other investments. From the employee standpoint, company stock is the investment the employee knows best and so may be attractive to people who either do not want to spend the time to learn about alternatives or have a strong belief in their own company. Balanced against these advantages, of course, must be an appreciation on both the part of the employee and the company that a failure to diversify a retirement portfolio is very risky.

For closely held companies, 401(k) plans are less appealing, although very appropriate in some cases. If employees are given an option to buy company stock, this can often trigger securities law issues most private firms want to avoid. Employer matches make more sense but require the company to either dilute ownership or reacquire shares from selling shareholders. In many closely held businesses, the first may not be desirable for control reasons and the second because there may not be sellers. Moreover, the 401(k) approach does not provide the "rollover" tax benefit that selling to an ESOP does, and the maximum amount that can be contributed is a function of how much employees put into savings. That will limit how much an employer can actually buy from a seller through a 401(k) plan to a fraction of what the ESOP can buy.

Despite these limitations, 401(k) plans are attractive as ownership vehicles in cases where a company simply wants employees to become owners but has no need to buy out owners or use the borrowing features of an ESOP. A company can simply match employee deferrals with company stock or make a straight percentage of pay contribution to all employees eligible to be in the plan in the form of company stock.

Accounting treatment is straightforward; any corporate contributions are charged to earnings, while employee purchases of shares add to shareholder capital.

Designing an Equity Incentive Plan

Designing an individual equity plan requires a variety of issues to be considered. This section is not intended to provide specific guidelines on how to structure a plan but rather to raise the issues companies need to consider. In making these decisions, company leaders should consult with peers and advisors, as well as evaluating available survey data on industry practices.

How Much to Share

The first decision is how much ownership to share. This issue will differ for closely held companies and public companies, so each kind of company is looked at separately.

Closely Held Companies

Except in an ESOP, where the goal is to sell stock to the plan, the most typical way a decision is made about how much ownership to share in a closely held company is for the current owner or owners to set aside an amount of stock that is within the maximum dilution level with which they are comfortable. This approach can create problems, however.

Typically, once this number is set, a large portion of those shares is either provided immediately to existing employees, or the shares are allocated to employees over a certain number of years. The problem with this strategy is that if the company grows faster than anticipated, there are no or relatively few shares left to give to new employees. That can be a severe problem in attracting and retaining good people. It can also create two classes of employees, some with large equity grants and some without them. Moreover, this model often does not create an explicit linkage between employee effort and the rewards of ownership.

A second approach focuses on what percentage of compensation is necessary to provide in the form of equity in order to attract, retain, and motivate people. These decisions need to be based on a sense of what people can get elsewhere, as well as discussions with employees to get a sense of how much they expect.

Rather than thinking about "how much" in terms of a total percentage of company shares or total compensation, it might make sense to use a more dynamic model based on performance. In this approach, the issue for existing owners is not "what percentage of the company do we own?" but "how much is what we own worth?" Owners in this model would rather own 10% of a $10 million company than 90% of a $1 million company. This notion can be made into an explicit plan by telling employees that if the company meets or exceeds certain targets, they will get a percentage of the incremental value created by that performance in the form of options. If the company exceeds its goals, then, by definition, sharing part of the surplus value leaves both the employees and the existing owners better off than they would have been. The targets can be anything: sales, profits, market penetration, or whatever else is critical to the company's future.

Finally, it should be noted that closely held companies need to consider the potential impact of equity grants to so many employees that they create legal or regulatory problems. An S corporation, for instance, cannot have more than 100 shareholders, and option holders count as shareholders. If any corporation has 500 or more shareholders (an ESOP or 401(k) plan only counts as one, however) and more than $10 million in assets, it becomes a *de facto* public company. Finally, equity plans may be subject to securities laws. This issue is described in more detail below in the section on securities law considerations.

Publicly Traded Companies

Publicly traded companies face many of the same design issues as their closely held counterparts, and may want to use some of the same decision guidelines. Their principal constraint is investor concern about dilution. Dilution is usually measured by "overhang," the number of awards outstanding plus the number of shares available to be issued. This amount varies by company. In broad-based equity plans, we found that most companies fall in the 5% to 25% range, with very large public companies often in the lower end of the range and technology companies and younger companies in the higher end.

What Kind of Equity?

ESOPs are the vehicle of choice if a company wants to use ownership sharing for business continuity. These plans also make sense in companies that have a strong commitment to sharing ownership broadly and find the ESOP rules acceptable given the tax benefits the plans provide. ESOPs do not work for companies that want to discriminate in terms of who gets awards or (in most cases) where the philosophy is that employees should have to buy stock to become owners. 401(k) plans make sense for companies that just want to share ownership broadly, are comfortable with the allocation rules, and, where employees are buying company stock, want to provide a tax-favored way for employees to invest. Generally, ESOPs and 401(k) plans are not means to provide incentives for individual behavior; instead, they are more targeted at providing incentives for employees as a group. ESPPs are a terrific benefit, but only a few companies will have active or substantial enough participation to make them a key element of their ownership cultures on their own. They are also less an incentive plan than a way to reward employees.

Very small companies with no plans to be acquired or go public often want to use SARs or phantom plans because they are simple, do not require actual stock to be issued, and can be used to track equity changes in non-stock companies. They lack some of the connotation of ownership, however, and offer no favorable tax treatment. Stock options and restricted stock, by contrast, require that the company provide some form of liquidity for the shares, often through a public offering or sale, although companies can also simply arrange to repurchase the shares.

Restricted stock and restricted stock units deliver actual shares to employees, even if the stock price declines. There are pros and cons to this approach. On the one hand, employees do not end up with nothing just because share prices decline in the market generally. On the other hand, some have argued that restricted stock just provides "equity for breathing," and that they are thus less of an incentive than options or SARs. Restricted stock can cause more economic dilution than either plan (because options are only exercised if the price of the stock goes up), but they cause less dilution in terms of the number of shares outstanding. That's because the risk protection of restricted stock means that each share granted is worth more than each option or SAR. A ratio of one restricted stock share to three or four stock options is not uncommon, for instance.

Option plans can be just NSOs, just ISOs, or some of both. Most broad-based option plans provide NSOs for rank-and-file employees because few of these employees will be able or want to meet the buy-and-hold conditions of the ISO. Many of those who do want to hold onto the shares, moreover, will not get a large benefit from being able to pay capital gains taxes rather than ordinary income tax rates. Because the employees will not use the benefits of an ISO anyway, companies reason they might as well get the tax benefit of an NSO.

On the other hand, many plans aimed at highly paid employees are ISOs because these employees can greatly benefit from capital gains treatment, and they may demand such options to come to work for or stay with a company. All-ISO plans are also common in start-up companies where the company is not worried about tax deductions (because there are no profits) and thus is willing to give all employees the benefit of the doubt on the possibility of getting capital gains treatment on their options.

Who's Eligible and Who Will Actually Get Equity?

In the past, the answer to the question of who is eligible was very simple for most companies: just our "key" people. In some ways, this is still how companies view equity; it's just that their definition of "key" has changed. For many companies, everyone is a key person. Many companies are pushing down more decision making to all levels of the company, asking employees to make business decisions on a regular basis. Management at these companies reasons that if they want people to think and act like owners, they should make them owners. At the same time, for some companies in some labor markets, it is necessary to provide options at all levels just to attract and retain people.

For companies in these situations, the answer to "who's eligible?" is simple: everyone is. Other companies choose a more complex approach, however. There are several criteria that can be considered in making this decision. This discussion is only for plans other than ESOPs, 401(k)s and ESPPs, where there are specific rules about eligibility. The sections that follow also will only be about individual equity plans, as these decisions are very constrained in ESOPs, 401(k)s, and ESPPs.

Tenure

At the simplest level, companies can require that people only can get equity after they have worked a minimum amount of time, often one year. This assures at least some commitment on the part of the employee to the company.

Full-Time/Part-Time

In the past, it was unusual to provide equity to part-time employees. Innovators like Starbucks, however, have provided options to everyone, arguing that many of their part-time people would (or if properly rewarded could) be long-term employees.

When Equity Will Be Granted

Equity can be granted either according to some kind of merit judgment or on the basis of a universal rule, such as allocating annually or on the date of hire, promotion, or the achievement of an individual, group, or corporate objective. These methods are not mutually exclusive; many companies use a combination of these techniques.

A typical merit-based plan would provide work unit managers (or a single manager in a smaller company) with a number of awards that can be granted to employees in the group based on a performance appraisal. An alternative to individual merit judgments is to provide that a pool of equity awards will be given to a work team on the achievement of their own goals. Many companies, of course, will simply name specific individuals, usually top managers, who will get equity, but define how much they get based on some merit assessment.

At the other end of the spectrum is an automatic formula based on compensation, seniority, promotion, or some other work-related, measurable construct. This can be for one employee or every employee. For instance, a number of larger companies provide all employees meeting basic service requirements with 10% of pay every year in stock options. The argument behind these formulas is that compensation reflects management's judgment of an employee's contribution to the company, and equity is simply another form of compensation.

Providing awards on hiring, with additional grants on promotion or periodic refresher grants, is another common allocation rule. Linking additional grants to promotion gives employees an incentive to improve their skills and rewards those people the organization believes are making greater contributions. On the other hand, it can lose the attention of employees who may be very good performers but who are not in jobs that can easily lead to a promotion.

Refresher grants give employees additional awards when they exercise some of the options or other equity benefits they were previously granted. For instance, if an employee has 1,000 options and exercises 200, then the employee would be given new options on another 200 shares at exercise. The theory here is to maintain a constant level of equity interest in the company. Similarly, refresher awards might be granted when the company issues additional shares so that an employee maintains the same percentage of potential ownership as was held prior to the dilution (this feature would be more common for executive plans). While these automatic additional grants help to keep the employee's equity interest high, shareholders might object to the ongoing dilution.

How Often Should Awards Be Granted?

Equity inherently involves risk, but the design of plans can accentuate that risk. Companies that provide one-time grants or grants on the attainment of an event, such as hiring, promotion, or meeting some corporate target, place most or all of an employee's ownership interest in the company based on the price of stock at a single point in time.

This practice accelerates the risk of equity both for the employee and the company. With options and SARs particularly, equity granted at a high price may never be "in the money"; awards given at a low price may cost the company more than it ever intended when they are redeemed. Employees who happen to get their chunk of equity at a good time end up doing very well, while those who have gotten their grants when the price was not so favorable don't do well at all. Creating an ownership culture of "we're all in this together" can be very difficult in these circumstances.

For many companies, the best way to deal with these potential problems is to provide grants in smaller amounts but more frequently. This works best for companies using equity as a compensation strategy. Start-ups whose stock value is close to zero anyway or that use large initial grants to attract people away from other opportunities may find this less appropriate. It also won't work for companies that want simply to make grants at the occasional discretion of the company, often on the attainment of some corporate milestone. These companies see equity more as a symbolic reward than as ongoing ownership strategy.

Smaller but more frequent grants are easiest to do in public companies where the share price is readily ascertainable and where share prices change continually. In a closely held company, there would be no point in granting equity more frequently than the stock is valued. Giving an employee a grant three times a year when the price per share is determined annually, for instance, would give the employee three sets of awards all at the same price.

The periodic allocation "dollar cost averages" the awards, smoothing bumps in volatile markets. This approach also gives employees more of a long-term, ongoing stake in the company. With the vesting schedules attached to the repeated grants of awards, employees are provided an even longer-term interest in the company's performance. Finally, there will be fewer big winners and losers among employees with otherwise similar jobs.

Frequent grants are not all good news, of course. The more often awards are granted, the more complex their administration becomes. Even with the best software, there will be much more data entry, many more forms to file and disseminate, and many more errors that can be made.

When Will Employees Be Able to Use the Awards?

There are two principal issues in deciding when employees will be able to translate their equity into cash: vesting and exercise periods. Vesting generally provides that an employee accrues an increasing right to the awards granted based on the number of years worked. However, companies also sometimes use performance vesting, in which vesting is a function of company, group, or individual performance. As various targets are met, the equity awards become increasingly vested. (Note that performance vesting triggers variable accounting for options and restricted stock, however.) The exercise period allows the employee to exercise or redeem an award for a defined number of years into the future once the award is vested.

The patterns on seniority-based vesting are fairly consistent across companies, with three- to five-year graduated vesting the most common schedule. Sales or profit targets are the most common performance triggers. A more difficult decision is whether to provide for immediate vesting upon an event, such as going public or sale, even if the awards would not otherwise be vested. This clearly provides a good benefit for employees, but it may make it more difficult to sell a company or take one public, especially if buyers perceive that employees will now have fully vested options that, if they can also then be exercised, may be valuable enough so that some people will just walk away.

By far the most common exercise period for stock options is 10 years; there are no data on other plans. Some exercise periods are shorter, but they are rarely longer. There is nothing magical about 10 years for nonqualified options, but for incentive options, the exercise period cannot exceed 10 years. The more volatile a company's stock, the more important a longer exercise period is so that employees can weather the downturns. An alternative design used by a few companies allows employees to exercise their awards only when a defined event occurs, such as the achievement of a certain stock price or earnings goal. This accomplishes two things. First, it provides an incentive to meet the goal, and secondly, it reassures investors that dilution will only occur if the company meets certain targets. Once these targets are met, employees would normally be given a certain amount of time after the event to exercise the award, anywhere from a few months to several years. Alternatively, a company could provide that awards can only be exercised upon the attainment of an event, such as a sale or going public.

In closely held companies, allowing exercise of an option or the right to sell shares only upon sale of the company or going public is a very common approach. If a company allows exercise and/or sale before then, employees end up owning stock and having a tax obligation. Unless the company can provide a market for the shares (an issue discussed below), this combination may not seem like much of a reward. Companies and employees have to weight just how likely these events are to occur, however. Management is often excessively optimistic about how marketable a company is.

It is also important to consider, as with vesting, that if employees can exercise on sale or an IPO, buyers of the stock may not find the company so valuable. A minority of closely held companies are thus now restricting exercise to some time after a sale or an IPO (in a sale situation, this would require the acquiring company to provide options in the new employer).

Finally, the plan design should be specific in its compliance with applicable securities laws and stock exchange rules that can restrict certain employees from exercising equity awards or the sale of stock acquired from them for a specified period after an IPO.

Providing a Market for the Shares

For publicly traded companies, providing a market for shares obtained through equity awards is not an issue, but for employees of closely held companies, it is one of the most important of all design issues. The majority of closely held companies solve the problem by limiting the exercise of equity awards to when the company is sold or goes public. This makes sense for companies that realistically see these alternatives as likely to happen in the foreseeable future. Some company leaders, however, assume that they can *only* provide for marketability upon these events because a closely held company, for one reason or another, cannot provide a market itself. There are, in fact, other alternatives. Moreover, some companies prefer to stay closely held. There are a variety of ways these companies can provide a market, including purchases by other employees (the company may act as a clearinghouse to let people know who is selling and who is buying), having the company buy back the shares, setting up an employee stock ownership plan (which can buy the shares with pre-tax dollars through an employee benefit trust) or, for companies willing to jump through the many securities law issues involved, setting up an internal stock market in which the company would act as a back-up buyer in a market is run for employee buyers and sellers.

Premium Pricing and Other Performance Bells and Whistles

Some companies are now looking at adding more performance triggers to their individual equity plans. As mentioned, vesting can be performance triggered, as can the actual grant of an award (or the size of that grant). In addition, companies can use premium priced awards, such as issuing an option at a grant price 10% above the current market price. In the executive compensation field, there are entire books written on formulas to base equity awards on performance. Another idea growing in popularity is indexed awards, where the award either only vests or is granted if the company's stock outperforms its peers. The details of these approaches are beyond the scope of this book, however. Suffice it to say that a common problem is picking performance measures (EBITDA, economic value added, stock price growth, etc.) that do not really capture either what the executive can actually make happen or what is best for the company overall, or both.

Securities Law Issues

If employees are given a right to purchase shares, the offer is subject to securities laws. ESOPs and 401(k) plans are not subject to most securities law requirements unless employees have a right to buy shares. The trust serves as the shareholder of record in these plans, and its ownership counts as one shareholder no matter how many people participate in the plan.

The two key elements of securities laws are registration and disclosure. Registration means the filing of documents with the state and/or federal securities agencies concerning the employer whose stock is being sold. It requires a lot of complex paperwork, including the filing of audited financial statements, and fees often exceed $100,000. Registration also requires continuing reporting obligations to the federal Securities and Exchange Commission (SEC) and appropriate state agencies.

Disclosure refers to providing information to buyers about what they are getting, similar to, but frequently less detailed than, what would be in a prospectus. At times, there are specific state and federal rules about what needs to go in these documents, including objective discussions of risks, the financial condition of the firm, officers' and directors' salaries, and other information. In the absence of requirements for the registration of the securities, disclosure is intended to satisfy the anti-fraud requirements of federal and state laws.

Generally, offers to sell securities (stocks, bonds, etc.) require registration of those securities unless there is a specific exemption. In addition, corporations with 500 or more shareholders and more than $10 million in assets are considered public companies under federal law and must comply with the reporting requirements of the Exchange Act of 1934 even if they do not have to register under the Securities Act of 1933. (An exemption added by the SEC in 2007 allows companies to exclude holders of unexercised compensatory employee stock options from the 500-shareholder calculation if the company otherwise does not have to report under the Exchange Act.)

There are a number of exemptions from these rules. These are exemptions from registration; whenever stock is offered, it should include appropriate financial disclosure to satisfy anti-fraud rules.

The most important exemption is Rule 701. Under federal law, offers to a company's employees, directors, general partners, trustees, officers, or certain consultants (those providing services to a company similar to what an employer might hire someone to do, but not consultants who help raise capital) can be made under a written compensation agreement. If total sales during a 12-month period do not exceed the greater of $1 million, 15% of the issuer's total assets, or 15% of all the outstanding securities of that class, then the offerings are exempt from registration requirements. The offerings must be discrete (not included in any other offer) and are still subject to disclosure requirements. For total sales under $5 million during a 12-month period to the specified class of people above, companies must comply with anti-fraud disclosure rules; for sales over this amount, companies must disclose additional information, including risk factors, copies of the plans under which the offerings are made, and certain financial statements. These disclosures must be made to all shareholders.

For purposes of this rule, options are considered part of the aggregate sales price, with the option price defined as of the date of grant. In calculating outstanding securities for the 15% rule, all currently exercisable or convertible options, warrants, restricted stock, stock rights, and other securities are counted.

Other exemptions are available for sale to a limited number of accredited or sophisticated investors with appropriate information (these terms are legally defined and generally include officers, directors, and/or higher-income individuals); small offerings to 35 or fewer nonaccredited investors; offerings under $1.000,000; and offerings only to in-state residents if the offeror does 80% or more of its business and has 80% or more of its assets in-state.

These exemptions from registration are available under federal law. Some states track federal exemptions; some do not. Most states model their "blue sky laws" (the general name for state securities laws) on the Uniform Securities Act or the Revised Uniform Securities Act, which are partly based on federal law. Perhaps most importantly for offerings to employees, however, states that have a specific exemption parallel to the federal Rule 701 exemption (for offerings to employees) are the exception rather than the rule. State registration for such offerings may be needed, therefore, unless other exemptions are met.

Public companies cannot use Rule 701 for an exemption from securities law filings. Instead, most rely on Form S-8, a simplified registration form that can be used to comply with securities laws in conjunction with an offering of options. Public companies do not have to offer a formal prospectus to potential buyers, as closely held companies would. They are, however, required to provide information to employee stock purchasers about the company and its option plan. The S-8 form allows that to be done by reference to already available public documents.

Public companies must also make sure their plan design complies with trading restrictions that apply to corporate insiders. This requires the filing of various reports and the restriction of some trading activity, among other things. These issues are too technical for adequate discussion here. Public companies should consult with their legal counsel on these matters before designing a plan.

About the Authors

Rich Armstrong is the president of The Great Game of Business, Inc. He has over 18 years of experience in improving business performance through employee involvement, business literacy, open-book management, and employee ownership, with service as a consultant and as an executive at SRC Holdings Corporation (an employee-owned company for 25 years). As an employee owner at SRC Holdings, Rich worked at many of its 17 subsidiaries in a variety of leadership positions ranging from business development to operations. Today, along with a network of Great Game coaches, Rich helps businesses implement the unique open-book management approach successfully practiced at SRC Holdings.

Brad Hams is the founder and president of Ownership Thinking, a 15-year-old consulting and training firm dedicated to unleashing the potential of its client organizations through employee education and involvement.

Cathy Ivancic is a consultant for and co-owner of Workplace Development Inc., which provides education, communication and organizational services to ESOP-owned companies nationwide. Since 1985, she has helped hundreds of companies enhance the impact of their ESOP and develop an ownership culture.

Loren Rodgers is a project director at the National Center for Employee Ownership, where he specializes in research, communications, and best practices for employee ownership companies. Active in the field since 1995, he works with firms on technical training, group norms, survey assessment, plan design, and communicating about transactions. He speaks extensively and writes for academic, trade, and employee ownership publications in the U.S. and abroad on topics including employee motivation, open-book management, corporate governance, ESOP education, organization dynamics, and business literacy.

Corey Rosen is the NCEO's executive director. He cofounded the NCEO in 1981 after working for five years as a professional staff member in the U.S. Senate, where he helped draft legislation on employee ownership plans. Before that, he taught political science at Ripon College. He is the author or coauthor of many books and over 100 articles on employee ownership, and coauthor (with John Case and Martin Staubus) of *Equity: Why Employee Ownership Is Good for Business* (Harvard Business School Press, 2005). He was the subject of an extensive interview in *Inc.* magazine in August 2000; has appeared frequently on CNN, PBS, NPR, and other network programs; and is regularly quoted in the *Wall Street Journal,* the *New York Times,* and other leading publications. He has a Ph.D. in political science from Cornell University and serves on the advisory board of the Certified Equity Professional Institute. He also served on the board of directors of the Great Place to Work Institute, creator of *Fortune* magazine's "100 Best Companies to Work for in America" list.

About the NCEO

The National Center for Employee Ownership (NCEO) is widely considered to be the leading authority in employee ownership in the U.S. and the world. Established in 1981 as a nonprofit information and membership organization, it now has over 2,500 members, including companies, professionals, unions, government officials, academics, and interested individuals. It is funded entirely through the work it does.

The NCEO's mission is to provide the most objective, reliable information possible about employee ownership at the most affordable price possible. As part of the NCEO's commitment to providing objective information, it does not lobby or provide ongoing consulting services. The NCEO publishes a variety of materials on employee ownership and participation, holds dozens of seminars, conference calls, Webinars, and conferences on employee ownership annually, and offers a variety of online courses. The NCEO's work includes extensive contacts with the media, both through articles written for trade and professional publications and through interviews with reporters. It has written or edited several books for outside publishers. See below for information on membership benefits and fees. To join, see the order form at the end of this section, visit our Web site at www.nceo.org, or telephone us at 510-208-1300.

Membership Benefits

NCEO members receive the following benefits:

- The bimonthly newsletter *Employee Ownership Report,* which covers ESOPs, equity compensation, and employee participation.
- Access to the members-only area of the NCEO's Web site, which includes a searchable newsletter archive, a discussion forum, a database of service providers, and more.

- Substantial discounts on publications, online courses, and events produced by the NCEO.
- Free access to live Webinars and conference calls.
- The right to contact the NCEO for answers to general or specific questions regarding employee ownership.

An introductory NCEO membership costs $90 for one year ($100 outside the U.S.) and covers an entire company at all locations, a single professional offering services in this field, or a single individual with a business interest in employee ownership. Full-time students and faculty members who are not employed in the business sector may join at the academic rate of $40 for one year ($50 outside the U.S.).

Selected NCEO Publications

The NCEO offers a variety of publications on all aspects of employee ownership and participation. Below are some of our publications.

We publish new books and revise old ones on a yearly basis. To obtain the most current information on what we have available, visit us on the Web at www.nceo.org or call us at 510-208-1300.

Equity Compensation

- *The Decision-Maker's Guide to Equity Compensation* describes the various types of equity compensation, how they work, and how to decide how much to give and to whom.

  $35 for NCEO members, $50 for nonmembers

- *Beyond Stock Options* is a complete guide, including annotated model plans, to phantom stock, restricted stock, stock appreciation rights, performance awards, and more. Includes a CD with plan documents.

  $35 for NCEO members, $50 for nonmembers

- *Accounting for Equity Compensation* is a guide to the accounting rules that govern equity compensation programs in the U.S.

  $25 for NCEO members, $35 for nonmembers

- *Equity Compensation for Limited Liability Companies* describes how equity compensation works in an LLC and provides a model plan document.

  $25 for NCEO members, $35 for nonmembers

Employee Stock Ownership Plans (ESOPs)

- *Understanding ESOPs* is an overview of the issues involved in establishing and operating an ESOP.

  $25 for NCEO members, $35 for nonmembers

- *Selling to an ESOP* is a guide for owners, managers, and advisors of closely held businesses, with a particular focus on the tax-deferred Section 1042 "rollover" for C corporation owners.

  $25 for NCEO members, $35 for nonmembers

- *S Corporation ESOPs* introduces the reader to how ESOPs work and then discusses the legal, valuation, administrative, and other issues associated with S corporation ESOPs.

  $25 for NCEO members, $35 for nonmembers

Other

- *The Handbook of Incentive Compensation* provides a broad look at motivating employees with both cash and equity.

  $25 for NCEO members, $35 for nonmembers

- *The Journal of Employee Ownership Law and Finance* is the only professional journal solely devoted to employee ownership. Articles cover ESOPs, equity compensation, and related subjects in depth.

  One-year subscription (four issues):
  $75 for NCEO members, $100 for nonmembers

To join the NCEO as a member or to order publications, use the order form on the following page, order online at www.nceo.org, or call us at 510-208-1300. If you join at the same time you order publications, you will receive the members-only publication discounts.

Order Form

This book is published by the National Center for Employee Ownership (NCEO). You can order additional copies online at our Web site, www.nceo.org; by telephoning the NCEO at 510-208-1300; by faxing this page to the NCEO at 510-272-9510; or by sending this page to the NCEO at 1736 Franklin Street, 8th Floor, Oakland, CA 94612. If you join as an NCEO member with this order, or are already an NCEO member, you will pay the discounted member price for any publications you order.

Name

Organization

Address

City, State, Zip (Country)

Telephone Fax Email

Method of Payment: ❑ Check (payable to "NCEO") ❑ Visa ❑ M/C ❑ AMEX

Credit Card Number

Signature Exp. Date

Checks are accepted only for orders from the U.S. and must be in U.S. currency.

Title	Qty.	Price	Total

Tax: California residents add 9.75% sales tax (on publications only, not membership)

Shipping: In the U.S., first publication $5, each add'l $1; elsewhere, we charge exact shipping costs to your credit card, plus a $10 handling surcharge; no shipping charges for journal subscriptions or membership

Introductory NCEO Membership: $90 for one year ($100 outside the U.S.)

Subtotal	$
Sales Tax	$
Shipping	$
Membership	$
TOTAL DUE	$